101 WAYS TO STOP ANXIETY

101 WAYS TO STOP ANXIETY

Practical Exercises to Find Peace and Free Yourself from Fears, Phobias, Panic Attacks, and Freak-Outs

TANYA J. PETERSON

Racehorse Publishing

TABLE OF CONTENTS

Introduction

"The best way out is always through." —Robert Frost

Anxiety is a snare, a suffocating and confining trap. Anxiety, worry, and fear usurp your thoughts and emotions and dictate your actions. When this happens, people often feel as though their lives are severely limited. What is your anxiety doing to you? (Check all that apply.)

- ☐ I can't stop thinking about things that have happened in the past.
- ☐ I'm worried about what is going to happen in the future, whether it's tomorrow or years down the road.
- ☐ I feel tired, but wired.
- ☐ I often just shut down.
- ☐ I have lots of vague, nagging thoughts.
- ☐ I have a small number of specific, intense worries.
- ☐ I feel crushed.
- ☐ I avoid people and situations.
- ☐ I feel stuck.
- ☐ I've tried to get rid of it, but my anxiety won't go away.
- ☐ My relationships are suffering.
- ☐ My work is suffering.
- ☐ I am suffering.

Whether you've checked one box or all of them, you're in a perfect place to begin to move right through your anxiety, past it, and onward to the life you desire. Forward movement is at the heart of this book.

The 101 tips, tools, and techniques you're about to learn come from researchers, practitioners, and people living with anxiety. I've used them myself when moving past my own strong anxiety, and I've helped others of all ages and backgrounds discover tools that help them move out of anxiety's vise. You'll see that I use "we" through-out this book—I'm one among millions of us who experience or have experienced anxiety.

While each of the tips inside is effective, you'll have some that you like better than others. Everyone is unique and therefore the ways they experience anxiety are, too; what works wonderfully for one person might not work well for the next. With patience, practice, and persistence, you'll discover your favorites.

The most powerful tool among all of these is actually number 102: You. *You* will be the one completing the actions and getting rid of anxiety.

Let's break out of anxiety's snare and into a life of well-being!

Section 1:
OVERTHINKING EVERYTHING TO DEATH

Anxiety is like a broken emergency broadcast system. It blasts screaming thoughts into your head: worries, assumptions, what-ifs, worst-case scenarios, and negative beliefs. Further, the emergency broadcasts never stop. Anxious thoughts keep coming—relentlessly.

In this section, you'll acquire ways to muffle anxiety's broadcast system so you can stop that anxious overthinking and free your mind for better thoughts.

1. I'm Having the Thought That . . .

ANXIETY LIKES TO RUN THROUGH the mind like it owns the place. It's possible to have multiple anxious thoughts running through your head at once, which means they dominate what you think about. Your anxious thoughts seem very real, and it's easy to stay caught up in them. Putting some distance between you and your anxious thoughts helps stop anxiety in its tracks.

The human mind is incredible. You can think many things, even things that aren't real. Close your eyes for a moment and think about a squirrel outside your window. Now, picture it to be six feet tall. And purple. It's carrying your favorite dessert, and it comes to the window to share with you.

Now, open your eyes. Chances are, your mind made that squirrel seem real. However, you didn't actually believe that the squirrel was real because you knew that this was just an exercise. You were aware that you were having *thoughts* about the giant purple squirrel with people treats. You can use this idea to your advantage to stop anxiety when you're overthinking.

When your thoughts are racing with worries and other negative beliefs and you feel like you're going crazy, take away their power by playing "I'm having the thought that . . ." If you're afraid of rodents and worried that a gigantic squirrel is going to show up in your yard bearing desserts, remind yourself, "I'm having the thought that a monstrous sugar-carrying squirrel will appear in my yard. It's just a thought." Then, turn your attention to what you are doing in the moment.

In the space between you and your anxious thoughts lies peace. Acknowledge the thought as merely a thought, then go about living in your present moment. Do this repeatedly, and your space will expand to help stop anxiety.

ACTION STEP TO TAKE NOW

List three anxious thoughts that frequently bother you. Rewrite each one using the "I'm having the thought that . . ." pattern. How will reframing your thoughts this way help reduce anxiety?

2. What if? Imagine the Possibilities!

SOMETIMES, ANXIETY CAN CONTROL YOU with two short words: "What if?" The words themselves aren't a problem; indeed, those words can bring exciting possibilities ("Hey, look at those birds. What if people could fly like that?").

"What if?" isn't a bad question. The problem isn't the question. Questions represent curiosity, learning, and growth. The problem is that anxiety creates anxious responses. Anxiety answers its own "what-ifs" in ways that make you worry even more. In response to the question, "What if I mustered the courage to sign up for that art class?" anxiety could immediately fill your thoughts with disastrous possibilities and reasons why you shouldn't pay good money to sit with other people trying to be creative. Anxiety can whitewash your dreams.

Take back your thoughts by interrupting anxiety with possibilities of your own. The next time anxiety starts putting worries in your head with its questions and immediate negative answers, grab a notebook and a pen and disrupt your anxious thoughts. For example, you didn't make it to your daughter's game because you were stuck in a meeting. Anxious thoughts begin. "What if I let her down and she's disappointed? What if I damaged our relationship?"

- First, answer over-the-top of anxiety with ideas of your own. Don't worry about being realistic. In fact, the more outlandish your answers, the better. Humor and the absurd switch the direction of our thoughts away from anxiety. You might write that your daughter will run away with the circus, she might disown you and throw you out of the house, and other answers that will throw off your anxious thoughts.

- Then, imagine the real possibilities. What are all of the good things that might happen in this situation? *What if* your work dedication will lead to a raise or a promotion? *What if* you can foster closeness by taking your daughter out to dinner and listening to her stories of the game? *What if* you're being a great role model for her? Imagine, and list, the possibilities.

When anxiety asks, "What if," reclaim your own thoughts by imagining the possibilities and answering boldly. Imagine how brightly, unburdened by anxiety, you'll paint your canvas.

3. Breathe Slowly, Deeply, Intentionally

YOU ARE EQUIPPED WITH YOUR own anxiety-reducing system: your breath. Breathing purposefully is a powerful way to reduce anxious thoughts and enhance well-being.

Where the breath goes, the mind will follow; where the mind goes, the breath will follow. When our breathing is rapid and shallow, our brain and body don't receive the right amount of oxygen needed to function properly and feel well. Shallow breathing creates tension and agitation. Anxious thoughts often follow. It works the other way, too. When you're experiencing anxiety and are overthinking things, your breath becomes more rapid and shallow. Most of us don't automatically recognize this action-reaction relationship between anxiety and the breath, but everyone can learn to recognize it and hone it to keep the mind calm and anxiety at bay.

First, learn how you typically breathe. At random times, place your hand over your chest and tune in to the rhythm of your breath. Then, begin to catch yourself breathing too rapidly. If you're feeling stressed, place a hand on your chest and notice the rise and fall of your breath. How does it compare to the baseline you established when tuning in to your breath at neutral times? Once you're aware of your breathing, take charge of it to create well-being.

The solution that can drastically reduce anxiety is to breathe intentionally. When your mind is running away with anxious thoughts and worries, stop what you're doing as soon as practical and pay attention to your breath. Purposefully take deep breaths. Inhale slowly for as many counts as you can. Pause. Exhale slowly for the same number of counts or even a couple more. Repeat.

Connect your thoughts with your breathing. Focus on slowly counting while inhaling and exhaling. Concentrate, too, on the sound and feeling of your breathing. Your mind will try to think anxious thoughts. Don't fight or focus on those thoughts. Just gently redirect them to your breath. The brain and body will receive oxygen, your muscles will relax, your mind will quiet, and anxiety will drop.

To have a long-term effect on anxiety, make intentional breathing a regular daily practice in your life.

ACTION STEP TO TAKE NOW

Learn Nodi Shodhana (Alternate Nostril Breathing)

This deep breathing exercise balances the oxygen in both hemispheres of the brain and can calm stress and anxiety. Try it now:

1. Sit comfortably, with your spine straight and your left hand resting in your lap.
2. Lift your right hand to your face and place your index and middle fingers between your eyebrows. Hover your thumb and ring finger above your nostrils.
3. Press your thumb against your right nostril to gently close it. Inhale slowly in through your left nostril.
4. Pause at the top of the inhale. Close your left nostril with your ring finger, let your right nostril open, and exhale through your right side.
5. Inhale through your right nostril, pause at the top, close the right side and open the left, and exhale completely through the left.
6. Repeat this pattern for several cycles.

Making Nodi Shodhana a daily practice will induce long-term anxiety-reducing benefits.

4. Make a Thought Jar

A THOUGHT JAR IS A collection of distractions—ideas to derail anxiety and shift your mind to something else. It's a useful tool to have when you're trying to fill your mind with something, anything, other than anxiety.

Anxiety causes us to ruminate or run our thoughts through our mind *ad nauseum*. We agonize over a familiar group of worries, overthinking and overanalyzing and getting stuck in deeply entrenched anxious thoughts. One way to overcome anxious thinking is to change what you're thinking about.

When you're anxious, though, it's hard to come up with other things to think about. Anxious thoughts seem to be the default setting in the brain. You can get around this by compiling a selection of completely random ideas that you can have on hand when you are stuck in anxious thoughts. Do this by creating and using a thought jar, thought box, thought notebook, or thought list in your phone.

You'll be collecting thoughts, so you'll need someplace to put them so you can conveniently access them. Choose what suits your personality and lifestyle. You might consider decorating your jar, box, or notebook because it's part of owning the process and making it pleasurable.

Next, create ideas to think about. Use slips of paper to stuff into a jar or box; otherwise, make lists. Jot down single words or phrases. For this purpose, you want a compilation of random ideas that you can turn to when you are overthinking: soccer, birds, cars, seasons, food, cities you want to visit—anything can be a thought topic (unless it's anxiety-provoking to you).

When you're stuck in anxious thinking, it's hard to pull the mind away and think about something else. With a collection of ideas, you can select one and immediately know what to think about. Start thinking about that topic in as much detail as you can. When the anxious thoughts creep back, redirect your thought to that topic. The more you do it, the better it works, and it will become natural to shift your attention away from your anxious thoughts.

5. Go Fishing without a Hook

FISHING WITHOUT A HOOK IS based on the Buddhist concept *shenpa*. *Shenpa* means "attachment," but renowned Buddhist nun Pema Chödrön refers to it as something stronger than attachment: getting hooked. When we are wrestling with anxious thoughts and over-thinking everything to such an extent that anxiety traps us, we are experiencing *shenpa*.

Imagine a fishing lure with a sharp hook. Sometimes, people accidentally hook themselves with the barbs. Because they're designed to snag and hold prey, fishing hooks embed themselves deeply. You can't (or shouldn't) just yank them out of your hand. Further, the more you thrash, the more deeply embedded the hook becomes. It's painful and can effectively end what could have been an enjoyable day of fishing.

Anxious thoughts are like fishing hooks. Once they catch your mind, you can't easily shake them loose. One way to avoid *shenpa* is by bypassing the hook in the first place. This visualization exercise trains your mind to evade hooks and negative thoughts.

Close your eyes and visualize a calm, clear lake. You're sitting in a boat, and you're fishing. Glance into the water and notice dozens of fish swimming about. Each has a sign that represents an anxious thought or worry you have. Picture yourself casting your line into the water again and again and catching nothing. You don't have a hook on that line, so the fish can't bite and hold—the thoughts don't stick.

As you do this exercise, breathe deeply and relax in the moment. Turn away from the fish and your thoughts and contemplate the peaceful lake setting. What does your mind see? What sounds are present? How does the air feel on your skin? Be detailed in your visualization. Enjoy your lake while your thoughts swim underneath you, unhooked. You're not consumed by your anxious thoughts because you're not experiencing *shenpa*.

It takes practice—many hookless fishing trips—but it's possible to unhook yourself from your thoughts. When you unhook yourself from anxious thoughts, you can propel your boat freely forward.

6. Go with the Flow

IT'S FRUSTRATING AND ALL TOO human. You've been busy, stressed out, keyed up with anxiety, and exhausted, and you're ready for some much-needed downtime. The moment you sit down to simply relax, though, your anxiety revs up and you resume overthinking and worrying. In fact, your thoughts are actually worse than they were before you tried to relax.

This is a very common part of anxiety. Worries, fears, and negative thoughts rush in to fill any void created when you take a break. Downtime can be more draining than work, school, and related tasks. You don't have to let anxiety ruin your relaxation. Anxiety might have been in charge of it for a long time, but no longer. You can take charge of both your free time and your own thoughts.

Dr. Mihaly Csikszentmihalyi, a professor and researcher in the field of positive psychology, teaches that *flow* is one of the biggest components of mental health and well-being. It's a state of being in which you are engaging in something so enjoyable that all thoughts, including anxiety, melt away. Your mind becomes focused yet still, lost in the activity yet very much found. In doing something that induces a state of flow, you stop worrying and ruminating and begin to enjoy your life.

Everyone has a different personality and a different set of interests, talents, and abilities; therefore, activities that fully immerse you will be unique to you. Consider it an exciting adventure to try different activities, hobbies, or volunteer opportunities to discover where you get lost in what you're doing. Aim for activities that are challenging enough to keep you interested but not so difficult that you become stressed and frustrated. Also, activities should be intrinsically rewarding. Pleasure should come from within. Flow happens when you benefit on the inside such as experiencing anxiety relief and calm thoughts. If you're doing something to look good or receive compliments, you probably won't create flow.

Downtime for stress and anxiety relief is crucial for mental health. Immersing your whole being in a positive activity flow will reduce anxious thoughts in the moment and over time.

ACTION STEP TO TAKE NOW

Grab some magazines and catalogs, a pair of scissors, some tape or glue, and some paper. Begin to discover where you could create flow by thumbing through the magazines and catalogs to find pictures of places and people doing things that seem fun to you. Cut them out, affix them to paper, and keep them for inspiration. Gather interesting images, and then pick one to try.

7. Color Your Thoughts

ANXIOUS THOUGHTS TAKE DIFFERENT FORMS. One such form is black-and-white thinking, a type of negative thought behind anxiety, depression, and other mental health challenges. Black-and-white thinking, also known as all-or-nothing thinking, is damaging. It causes anxiety, worsens existing anxiety, and makes people feel trapped in their anxiety.

When you catch yourself using words like "always," "never," or "every," you're probably engaging in all-or-nothing, anxious thinking. Other black-and-white thinking involves judgement words and phrases, such as, "I'm a terrible parent." This type of thinking is like tunnel vision for anxiety. Black-and-white thinking makes you believe that *all* your anxious thoughts are true and that things will *never* get better.

Change this thinking pattern to help reduce your anxiety. Fix your black-and-white thoughts by adding color.

Begin this exercise by reflecting on the black-and-white thoughts that are driving many of your worries. As you brainstorm, write the anxious thoughts in a journal, notebook, or computer document. Generate as many thoughts as you can. Even if you only think of a few right now, that's okay. Like all exercises in this book, Color Your Thoughts is meant to be repeated over time.

Next, choose one thought and write it in black ink at the top of a page. Now it's time to expand your thinking and create new possibilities. Using markers, colored pencils, or different colored fonts on your computer, list as many thoughts and possibilities as you can to disrupt the black-and-white thought. If you're working with the thought that you're a terrible parent, for example, you might list the things you do right, the ways you care for your children, signs that your children are happy and well-adjusted, and anything else positive about yourself, your parenting, and your children. Use a different color for each item on your list to reinforce the idea that you're adding colors to expand the spectrum of your thoughts and subsequently limit all-or-nothing thinking.

The more you do this exercise, the more aware you'll become of your black-and-white thoughts. As you expand your thinking, you'll grow past anxiety's limited thoughts. When this happens, you'll outgrow both automatic thinking and anxiety itself.

8. The Finger Trap: Accept Your Anxiety and Slip Past It

ACCEPTANCE AND COMMITMENT THERAPY (ACT) is a research-based approach to mental health and well-being, including anxiety reduction that teaches us to accept certain things in our lives. One such thing is our anxious thoughts. Doesn't that sound absolutely awful? Why would anyone want to accept anxiety? Doesn't that imply giving in and believing the thoughts? Despite what it sounds like initially, "acceptance" does not mean backing down to the anxious thoughts, giving up, and resigning oneself to living with anxiety. In the case of ACT, acceptance is a liberating mindset. Imagine a finger trap, one of those woven paper tubes into which you place each forefinger. If you've ever used these, you might recall that the harder you yank the trap, the tighter it becomes. You can't get out of the trap by struggling and fighting with it. It's the same with your anxiety.

Once again imagine the paper trap over your fingers. Take a slow, deep breath and relax. Rather than frantically pulling to break free from the trap, accept that the trap is over your fingers. Let it be there and gently move your fingers together. Watch the trap expand and slip your fingers out.

You can only extract yourself from the finger trap by accepting its presence and relaxing. When you accept your anxious thoughts, you don't believe them or accept their content. Instead, you simply accept the fact that right now, in this moment, anxious thoughts are present in your mind like a finger trap. That's it. You are having anxious thoughts and you acknowledge this as a neutral fact.

When you notice and accept that you're having anxious thoughts rather than struggling against them, you no longer focus on anxiety. Acceptance of anxiety allows you to turn your thoughts elsewhere and has the potential to bring a sense of inner peace. Accepting anxiety doesn't always come easily, so keeping a finger trap on hand can serve to remind you to develop inner peace by accepting anxiety's presence rather than focusing on it.

9. What Will You Put in Your Head to Replace Anxious Thoughts?

WHAT WILL YOUR LIFE BE like when anxiety is gone and your thoughts are calm and pleasant? Before reading on, take some time to thoughtfully answer the question in your notebook. Write, scribble, sketch, tape pictures—answer this question in a way that is meaningful to you. This is a chance to dare to dream of the quality life you are creating. How will your relationships change when anxious thoughts aren't a third wheel? What about work? Home? Activities? Lifestyle? What thoughts will fill your mind?

Envisioning your anxiety-free mind is an important part of reducing anxious thoughts. Trying to vanquish anxiety doesn't work if you don't have something with which to replace those anxious thoughts. Imagine you have a hole in your yard. Every day, your sprinklers fill that hole with water. The water attracts mosquitos, so every day you go outside and scoop the water out of the hole. It's a big hole, so it takes a lot of your time and energy. Then the very next day, the sprinklers start up and once again fill the hole.

This annoying cycle will continue to consume your life unless you do something to change what occupies that hole. Perhaps you might plant a tree or a rose bush—something that replaces the hole and the water and brings beauty and pleasure to your life.

What will you put in your head to replace anxious thoughts? Reflecting on these questions can help you begin to replace your anxious thoughts with better things. Using your notebook, record your answers to the following questions:

- When you're not thinking anxious thoughts, what do you think about?
- When have you felt the freest from your anxious thoughts?
- What would go on in your mind if anxious thoughts weren't so intense?
- What would you be able to do differently if anxiety weren't holding you back?

Thoughtfully responding to these questions helps you set goals for what you want in anxiety's place. Don't just scoop water out of a muddy hole. Plant beauty and help it thrive.

ture Your New Thoughts

WOULD 'T IT BE WONDERFUL IF we could simply think a new, better, non-anxious thought and have it automatically take hold? If you've tried this, you might already know that, unfortunately, it doesn't work this way. The reason new thoughts don't instantly replace old, anxious ones is because they must be nurtured so they grow and fill your mind, pushing out anxious, negative thoughts.

As you replace anxious thoughts with new, positive ones, it's important to cultivate them with your attention. Try these strategies for nurturing your new thoughts:

- **Recognize and remember positive thoughts.** It can feel as though anxiety has control of all your thoughts, but when you take time to notice, you'll see that you think things that have nothing to do with anxiety. Notice when your thoughts aren't consumed by anxiety and jot down those thoughts. Simply knowing that not everything is anxiety-based can be encouraging and motivating.

- **Stop copying anxiety's focus.** Anxiety focuses on problems, and when you do, too, the problems are magnified. Let anxiety go on trying to create anxious thoughts. You turn to focusing on creating solutions to what anxiety is drumming up.

- **Use your positive thoughts and ideas to shape tangible, manageable goals.** Let your thoughts and ideas for solutions to anxiety-driven problems move you forward. One reason new thoughts don't instantly replace anxious ones is because they remain as intangible thoughts. When you use your new ideas to form goals for your anxiety-free life, positive reinforcement is at work. Creating and pursuing goals—and watching them manifest—reinforces the validity of positive thoughts. Success leads to more success as you continue to replace anxiety.

- **Once you have some goals (or even just a single goal to start), nurture those goals.** Create a step-by-step action plan for how you will accomplish them. With each step, you are taking action. You're reducing anxious thoughts and replacing them with reality-based thoughts that you have created and nurtured.

Replacing negative, anxious thoughts is empowering. Instead of remaining stuck in your anxious thoughts, you change them—and in the process, you change yourself and your life.

ACTION STEP TO TAKE NOW

Write down one new goal you'd like to cultivate, such as "I will pay attention to my daughter's softball game rather than worrying about what the other parents are saying and thinking about my daughter and me." Then, brainstorm what little things you will do to accomplish it.

11. Make a Mole Hill out of a Mountain

IT'S A FUNCTION OF THE human brain when anxiety is at work: we all make mountains out of mole hills. Officially, this is known as catastrophizing or magnification. Have you noticed that your anxiety makes almost everything loom large? When you're wrestling with anxiety, the slightest little thing—a comment, a look, an event, a situation—can instantly explode into mountainous proportions. This intensifies anxiety and can make your life seem impossible to deal with. (And yes, it can be your whole life that feels overwhelming. The magnification transferred from one situation to your life as a whole is your anxiety making a mountain out of a mole hill.)

The good news is that you can indeed deal with your life and any anxiety-provoking situation in it. The key is to take the mountains created by your anxious thoughts and turn them back into mole hills. Try this step-by-step process:

- **Step 1:** Notice when you are thinking about big problems and consequences. Pay attention to intense worries, what-ifs, and fears.

- **Step 2:** Stop what you're doing and take several slow, deep breaths to center yourself and calm your nervous system.

- **Step 3:** Identify what you're worried about. List your concerns on paper if it's practical. Set a timer for five minutes, and when it sounds, stop.

- **Step 4:** Now that the worries are out in front of you, break them apart. Just as a real mountain isn't one solid piece but is made of many different materials, so, too, is your mountain of anxious thoughts. Observe your worries as individual items rather than as one big chunk.

- **Step 5:** Now, start to reduce the mountain by making mole hills. Break the worries apart so they're more manageable.

- **Step 6:** Choose just one molehill, the worrisome thought that is bothering you most. Considering just that issue right now, what action steps can you take to minimize the problem even more?

- **Step 7:** Continue to reduce the mountain and all its molehills.

Making molehills out of these mountains is a process that takes work and time, but with patience and persistence, you will wear down your mountain of anxiety.

12. Live in Your Neutral Zone

ANXIOUS THOUGHTS LIVE IN OUR past and ruminate over what has already happened. Sometimes they race into the future, worrying about what might happen. They race back and forth between past and future, but they stay out of the neutral zone. The neutral zone is the present moment—the moment of your life right now. Anxious thoughts try to pull you back to the past or propel you into the future. You might over-think something that happened many years ago or just a few minutes ago. The same can be said for worries about the future. Maybe you're worrying about long-term outcomes of something going on now, or your anxiety might involve the fact that in just a minute you have to walk across the room and talk to someone. Regardless of what time period your anxiety carries you to, the subject of anxious thoughts is always the past or the future.

Living within your neutral zone, the present moment, can help reduce anxiety and anxious thoughts. This strategy is known as mindfulness, and it allows you to let go. Mindfulness encourages you to turn away, dismissing your anxious thoughts with a flick of a wrist.

Replace your worries with thoughts of what is happening in this moment. Your senses are built-in tools for this. What do you see? Hear? Feel? Smell? Taste? Carry interesting items with you that you can study and touch. Have gum or mints on hand. Look around you and simply observe everything with your senses. Think about tangible things that are around you right now.

The neutral zone doesn't lie in a vacuum. Notice that when you live in the neutral zone and focus on what is going on right now, you're not doing anything to avoid or eradicate your anxious thoughts. The thoughts continue to circle and race; however, you're not paying attention to them. By grounding yourself in the present moment, you take away anxiety's power over you. Rather than dwelling on anxious thoughts, you're engaged in the present moment. This means that you're living your life, moment by moment, even if anxiety isn't fully gone. The more you inhabit your neutral zone, the more your mindful thoughts will replace anxious thoughts.

13. Stop *Shoulding* on Yourself

HOW OFTEN DO YOU USE the word "should" when thinking about yourself or your life? Have you uttered statements like these?

- I should exercise more.
- I should stop eating fast food.
- I should work more.
- I should spend more time with my family.
- I should make more money.
- I shouldn't be so selfish.
- I should stop worrying so much.
- I should be better.
- I shouldn't be the way I am.

This is but a small list of things people tell themselves. In the world of psychology and counseling, statements like this are known as a type of cognitive distortion, a faulty thought pattern we think is true. When psychologists and therapists hear people using—and believing—such bossy "should" statements, they often call them out for "*shoulding* all over themselves." Because, you know, *shoulding* is a pretty crappy thing to do to yourself.

"Shoulds" are anxious thoughts that cause a great deal of inner tension and stress. They're toxic bullies that prevent you from feeling good about who you are. They prevent you from moving forward into the anxiety-free, quality life that you desire.

"Should" statements are so deeply ingrained, developed from early childhood on, that it can be difficult to stop them. As with other aspects of anxiety, you don't have to stop the thoughts. The goal is to stop believing them or using them to define your worth. These five steps will help you stop "shoulding all over yourself:"

- **Identify:** Catch yourself using "should" statements.
- **Acknowledge:** With a matter-of-fact attitude, notice (without believing) the content and message of your "should" statement.

- **Question:** Why? For example, why "shouldn't" you have said that? Then question your answer: Why is that important? Keep going until you no longer have an answer to all of the "whys." Do your answers match your values and life goals?
- **Act:** Keep doing what you can and want to do to reach the goals you have set for yourself.

Learn not to listen to your "should" statements so you're no longer bullied by these anxious thoughts.

ACTION STEP TO TAKE NOW

Action step to take now

Identify one of the biggest "should" rules you impose on yourself. "Should" you be a better partner/friend/parent? Maybe you "shouldn't" eat fast food as often as you think you do. Now cross it out and replace the statement with one that shows that the "should" statement is inaccurate. You might state, "I am a parent who is more than good enough. I make time for my children and make sure they are safe, cared for, and heard."

---

14. Train Your Brain to Break Its Negativity Bias

THE HUMAN BRAIN IS WIRED to look for problems. It's been doing this for hundreds of thousands of years, so it has perfected the art. Not only does it look for problems, it's accomplished at finding them and worrying about them. Psychologists call this process and habit the negativity bias. Early in human history, this was a good thing—and to some extent, it still is. To stay safe and alive, we need to be alert for danger. In anxiety, however, the negativity bias becomes too powerful and a bad habit. You can train your brain to break that habit.

You're probably quite aware that you have negative and anxious thoughts, such as worrying about what you think you've done wrong while discounting what you've done right. It's possible, though, that you don't realize how much you watch for, and think about, possible problems. The first step in breaking the habit is to become aware of this negativity bias. Pay attention to what you watch for and think about. Notice your negative thinking patterns.

Next, seek, find, and think about other, more positive and realistic things. These techniques have been shown to be successful brain-training tools:

- **Keep a gratitude journal.** Intentionally look for things big and small that you appreciate. Record them in your journal and build a go-to list of positive ideas and thoughts. As you do this, you'll train your brain to break its negativity bias.

- **Celebrate the things that make you grateful.** Identify little things every day, maybe even multiple times a day, that you can pause and celebrate. Celebrations take many forms and can be as simple or elaborate as you wish. Do a happy dance. Play a favorite song. Take a quick, brisk walk. Take a ten-minute break to read a chapter in a good book. Draw a picture. Celebrating reinforces the positive in your life and is a great brain-training tool to reduce anxiety.

Habits are changed through action, patience (with yourself and with the process), and persistence. Breaking the negativity bias and training your brain to seek out the good is possible and life-changing.

15. Organize Mental Chaos with a Thought Log

REDUCING ANXIOUS THOUGHTS IS HARD when you don't know exactly what you're up against. When your thoughts seem to constantly race with anxious worries and what-ifs, how do you possibly stop the anxiety? Often, it helps to start by organizing the mental chaos.

When you live with anxiety, it's normal to have the feeling that "everything" is making you anxious; however, that isn't usually the case. A bit of sorting and organizing will help you know what is bothering you the most so you can deal with it, thus reducing anxiety. Charting your anxious thoughts will allow you to see them out in front of you instead of zooming and spinning, undefined, in your head. When you can analyze them, you can determine what thoughts you want to change and how you want to change them.

Start by writing down anxious thoughts. It's effective to jot them down while you're having them to capture them exactly as they are, but that's not always practical. It also works to have a time each evening when you reflect on your day and write down your anxieties.

Writing down your worries lets you better understand what you're anxious about, but there are other things that are necessary to know. Get specific. Like a journalist, chart the *who, what, where, when, why,* and *how* of each worry. Write down particular thoughts. Organize the information in a chart, graph, concept map, or list—any way that your brain prefers to make meaning.

Now that you can see your data, look for patterns so you can see what brings the greatest anxiety. Look for relationships, situations, and themes. Are your thoughts past- or future-oriented? When is your anxiety the worst? When is it better? Identify what's happening with your anxious thoughts and decide which ones to tackle first. Sometimes, people start with the most bothersome one. Other times, that feels too daunting, so people will start with smaller situations and thoughts to build success. You can personalize this entire process to suit you. This systematic, logical approach is effective in reducing anxiety.

16. Anxiety Focuses on Problems. You Focus on Solutions.

IN STRATEGY 14, YOU LEARNED about the negativity bias. The anxious brain constantly scans for danger and anything threatening or negative. This causes us to be problem-oriented. To stop anxiety, you can change your thinking to be solution-oriented.

Three important things to know about problems:

- A problem is only a true problem when it takes over and keeps you from moving forward to create a quality life.
- Even when it takes over your life, like anxiety often does, it's temporary because most problems have solutions.
- Therefore, even anxiety isn't a true problem. It isn't permanent. You can turn your attention to solutions to the anxiety in your life.

Solution-focused therapy is an approach to mental health, including anxiety reduction, that looks past problems. Instead of being stuck ruminating over your anxious thoughts, shift your thinking to developing solutions. The shift itself is liberating. It focuses on creating the inner strength to develop and implement the solutions to anxiety. Try these two approaches to stop anxiety with a solution mindset:

- Look for exceptions to the problem. It can feel like anxiety is always, always, in your thoughts. It does seem that way, but that's probably not reality. Pay attention on purpose and find those times when your thoughts aren't anxious (or are even just less anxious). What's going on then? How can you create more of these times of reduced anxiety?
- When you're plagued by anxious thoughts about what you did wrong or said wrong, ways in which you're not good enough, fears about "what might happen if . . . ," and other things that make you miserable, counter them. For every thought about something that's *wrong*, write down something that's *right*. It can be a direct counter to the anxious thought, or it can be something entirely different. The idea is to increase your awareness of things that aren't anxiety-provoking.

When you actively focus on solutions, exceptions, and what is right, you begin to detach yourself and your mind from anxiety. The less you focus on anxiety-related problems, the better able you'll be to look past anxiety and replace it.

ACTION STEP TO TAKE NOW

Create a time of reduced anxiety today (rather than "this weekend" or "after I finish this project." What do you in the evening when you're feeling less anxious? Plan to do that tonight. What will you do, who will be with you, and how long will you do it?

---

17. Do Some Research. Change How You Think About Yourself.

ONE PARTICULARLY NASTY EFFECT OF anxiety is that it makes us incredibly, even painfully, hard on ourselves. Anxiety typically brings harsh self-judgments in the form of labels and negative self-talk. Ponder for a moment how you think about yourself. How does your self-talk sound? Do you say things like "I'm an idiot," or "I'm going to screw up like always," or "I'm awful to be around?" Just because you have anxious, negative self-talk doesn't mean it's accurate. It's time to change how you talk to yourself.

The goal is to change the words you use to describe yourself. Harsh labels and anxious thinking increase anxiety and decrease your sense of self-worth. If you've been labeling yourself harshly, there's a good chance that you've come to believe the words. "I'm worthless" might feel more fitting than "I'm valuable."

Not only can you begin to describe yourself with positive labels, you can start believing them. Begin by paying attention to yourself. Notice things you do, talents you have, roles you take on, and how you interact with others. This might feel uncomfortable at first because people with anxiety don't want to pay attention to themselves. Observe yourself despite any discomfort.

Keep track of what you notice. Catch yourself being the person you want to be. Avoid the anxious tendency to find your faults and label them. When your mind goes there, neither argue nor listen; instead, turn gently back to seeking the good in yourself. Simply observe and gradually open your mind to the possibility that there's more to you than negative labels created by anxious thoughts.

The next step is to use your observations to change your thoughts about yourself. Either in column format or with a mind map, write down a negative, anxiety-based harsh label. Add a positive label, based on your observations, to counter it. Add examples to reinforce for yourself that this positive label is accurate. For example:

Negative, Anxiety-Based Label	Positive Label That Counters the Negative One	Examples That Show the Positive Label is Accurate
I'm annoying	I'm helpful	In yesterday's work meeting, I did talk a lot, but it was because I had ideas for a solution. My colleagues took my suggestion.

As you do this over time, your thoughts about yourself will change, as will your self-talk. Even when negative thoughts appear, they'll no longer bother you because you've replaced them with realistic, positive beliefs.

18. Reason with Your Thoughts

ANXIOUS THOUGHTS ARE OFTEN OUT-OF-CONTROL thoughts. They ricochet in your head, colliding and escalating. Sometimes, you need to be the voice of reason in your relationship with anxiety.

Reasoning with your anxiety is a way to help you deal with it logically. It's a process of reducing it to manageable bits and then deciding upon a course of action. Try this procedure:

- **Step 1:** List some of your most persistent and bothersome thoughts.
- **Step 2:** Choose just one to start.
- **Step 3:** Determine what is bothering you about the idea by breaking it down into small chunks. For example, worrying about going to an event because you're afraid you might embarrass yourself is both too big and too vague to easily handle. List things about the situation that are causing anxiety.
- **Step 5:** Question each item on your list. Ask such things as, "How would the embarrassment happen?", "What would happen to me because if it?", "What's the worst that could happen?", "How would it really affect me?", etc.
- **Step 6:** Consider your answers and list your options. What could you do about the event you're worried about? What reasonable steps can you take to address and handle the answers to your questions?
- **Step 7:** Decide the steps you need to take to move forward. Keep in mind that action steps don't have to be dramatic. Further, you might reason that, after looking at the individual components of your worries, you don't want to take any action now. What matters is that you've made a choice based on reason rather than on fear.
- **Step 8:** Act without second-guessing yourself. You've decided; now, follow through without worrying about whether it's right. You can move forward confidently because you have thoroughly considered and reasoned with your anxious thoughts.

This reasoning process can be effective because, in working through it, you pause to fully consider your anxiety. Listening to and questioning your thoughts leads to fresh insights. The more deeply you understand your fears and worries, the better you can handle anxious thoughts. As your anxiety improves, so, too, does your ability to live and think freely.

19. Affirm Your Self-Worth to Change How You Think About Yourself

YOU'VE LEARNED THAT YOU CAN change how you think about yourself by investigating the correctness of your thoughts. Sleuthing can be very effective in transforming our opinions about ourselves; however, sometimes anxiety causes such deeply ingrained self-loathing that we need to have additional tools to build self-acceptance. A helpful way to create thoughts about yourself that are more realistic is to regularly affirm your self-worth based on objective evidence.

Affirmations are short statements based on self-observation or observations about you made by others. To make affirmations work for you, write down as many positive things about yourself as you can. Think about accomplishments, strengths, character traits, abilities—anything you like about yourself, big or small. It might feel awkward at first to do this, and it might even be incredibly difficult. That's okay. Your anxious thoughts have probably been bullying you for quite some time, so this process won't come naturally. Just let it feel awkward and do it anyway.

As you write your affirmations, you can pair them with negative thoughts that are bothering you a great deal. If you have a recurring anxious thought like, "I can't do anything right and I'm going to lose my job," you can write affirmations that show how unrealistic this statement is. You could write statements such as:

- I'm always on time and people can rely on me.
- I'm creative and good with [complete the statement with work tasks].
- My boss thanks me for my hard work.

Write your affirmations and place them where you'll see them. Tape them to your mirror, your phone cover, the refrigerator, in drawers, or anywhere that you will see them. If you don't want others to see them, keep a stack of affirmations private but accessible so you can read them to yourself often.

Affirmations become part of your natural thoughts over time as you repeat them daily. You'll enjoy reduced anxiety and increased self-confidence as you replace your anxious, mean thoughts about yourself with positive, accurate statements.

ACTION STEP TO TAKE NOW:

Use a thesaurus to compile a variety of meaningful words you can use to describe yourself.

20. Let the Parade Go By

IF YOU'RE AWAKE, YOU'RE PROBABLY thinking. It's likely that worries and fears are a prominent part of your incessant thought parade. You have already learned that you have options for dealing with your anxious thoughts. You might change their content. You could choose different, more pleasant, things to do instead of struggling with your thoughts. You could build a different road to travel on rather than staying with the parade of thoughts. Or, you could sit back and just let the parade go by.

We can't control what thoughts pop into our heads as part of this ongoing procession. Further, sometimes there are so many anxious thoughts that we become easily overwhelmed. At times like these, an approach that comes from mindfulness is effective in calming your thoughts and reducing anxiety.

Wherever you are, whatever you're doing, give your undivided attention to the present moment. Take everything in with your senses and immerse yourself in your surroundings. Your parade of thoughts will continue, and that's okay. Let it go right on by. Thoughts will pop into your mind, but you don't have to give them your attention. Imagine them as parade floats and yourself as a distant spectator. It doesn't matter what anxious thoughts you have or how many or how quickly they come. Don't struggle with them or try to stop them, and they'll keep rolling.

As you let your thought parade pass by, breathe slowly and deeply. This increases your sense of calm and inner peace as it soothes the brain and nervous system. Deep breathing can even release tension as it helps muscles relax. The more relaxed and calm you become, the more easily it will be to be immersed in your present moment; thus, you'll be equipped to let your thoughts parade right on by.

This experience will help you increase your awareness of what is real and what isn't. The things that you can see, hear, smell, feel, and perhaps taste are tangible, and they comprise your real life. The thoughts that are marching by are merely ideas. They have no substance; therefore, let them pass by.

Section 2:
ANXIETY AT WORK OR SCHOOL

Work and school are naturally anxiety-provoking because they involve pressure and consequences. You must work with others and navigate their moods and attitudes. Often, you have people above you that have a part to play in your success or failure—anxiety-provoking indeed.

The following strategies will help you shift your outlook and actions to decrease anxiety and increase contentment at school or work.

21. *Good* Morning Ritual

A GOOD WORK OR SCHOOL day begins long before you arrive. Develop a morning ritual to start the day with peace and calm rather than worry and tension. It begins with getting out of bed, a task that can feel impossible when you have somewhere to go that makes you anxious. It's natural to avoid getting up but giving in to the urge strengthens anxiety as you imagine what lies ahead. It also robs you of time. You'll feel rushed and stressed so that by the time you get where you're going, anxiety is already in control.

You can take back control. Change your habit by developing a ritual. Lying in bed is nothing more than a behavior that has developed in response to anxiety. It isn't a weakness, a character flaw, laziness, or any other negative (and inaccurate) label you might have applied to it. To create a ritual to make good mornings, shift your thinking. You don't have to beat anxiety before you can easily get out of bed. That will come in time. First, start a new habit of getting up despite a sense of dread.

Your morning ritual might look like this:

- Tidy your living spaces the night before so you don't wake up to stress-inducing clutter.
- Place a glass of water beside your bed. When your alarm sounds, inhale deeply, stretch, sit up, and drink the full glass. Take your time and feel it begin to rehydrate you. This helps settle anxiety in your body.
- Leave your bedroom and go to a space you've set up for yourself. Sit quietly, mindful of the sights, sounds, and smells of the room as well as the feel of your body in the chair and feet on the rug. Take several slow, deep breaths. Enjoy a cup of tea or decaf coffee (caffeine can increase anxiety).
- When you're ready, slowly stand and continue to prepare for your day.

Feel free to spend as much or as little time as you'd like in this ritual and tailor it to your own life. Having a period of serenity before your day gets going will improve your mornings and reduce anxiety for your day.

ACTION STEP TO TAKE NOW

Decide what your morning ritual will be tomorrow (you can always adjust it as you determine what is most helpful). Prepare what you need for it this evening and write yourself a note with encouraging, motivating words to read as you get up.

22. Who Needs Perfection When You're Good Enough?

PERFECTIONISM CAUSES ANXIETY AND MISERY. It involves a deep-seated fear of failure and negative judgement, and it can be paralyzing. Your anxiety might be linked to perfectionism if:

- You find yourself second-guessing yourself so much that getting anything done seems impossible
- You worry about not measuring up to expectations
- You ruminate about your perceived shortcomings and are apprehensive about failure
- You dread the idea of being viewed as incompetent
- You find yourself comparing yourself to others and experiencing stress because you think you come up short
- After you complete a project, you obsess anxiously over what you could have done better
- It's hard for you to take pride in something you've done because you don't believe you've done well
- You have anxiety about not being good enough

Experiencing anxiety for being imperfect blocks you from feeling content and competent, which intensifies the drive for perfectionism. The fear of imagined consequences grows, causing even more anxiety. It's a painful cycle that you can break when you realize that you don't have to be perfect to be good enough. This exercise will help you expand your perspective. Use a journal or notebook to reflect:

- Describe where perfectionism is intruding in your life.
- What might happen to you if, in the situation you described, you made mistakes? Brainstorm and list as many possible consequences—positive and negative—as you can think of.
- Study your list. How would you respond to each possibility? How would you survive the bad?

- What would it be like for you if the pressure to be perfect disappeared and you could do your best, content that "good enough" really is good enough?

In reflecting on your anxieties, you're gently opening your mind to new thoughts and interpretations. Rather than using all-or-nothing thinking (either I'm perfect or I'm a failure), you can begin to see that there's a great deal of space between the extremes. The more you do this exercise, the more room you'll create to exist between perfection and failure. You'll realize that good enough is really pretty great.

23. Do You Isolate? Hide? Let These Lists Be Your Guide

IT CAN MAKE YOUR HEART beat hard and fast against your rib cage. It might put a giant lump in your throat, make your stomach burn and your ears feel hot. "It" is the thought of co-workers, supervisors, classmates, and teachers nearby. Anxiety often makes people feel tense, keyed-up, and sometimes even panicked when they feel scrutinized or forced to interact with others.

While it's tempting to keep your head down and isolate yourself, doing so increases anxiety over time because it makes it increasingly difficult to emerge from hiding and join in. Not only that, avoiding others prevents you from being fully present for a significant chunk of your life.

You don't have to remain separate and miserable. That said, you also don't have to plunge in and be the center of everything. Determine your own goal for coming out of hiding. To grow toward this goal without exacerbating anxiety, think in terms of your comfort zone. Inch up to the edge of it, then stretch yourself past it ever so slightly.

Do you want to talk to someone you know before a class begins? Do you want to speak up in a meeting? Ending isolation is daunting, but doable. Reduce anxiety about being brave by making some lists to guide you through the process.

- **List people.** Whom might you enjoy talking to?
- **List topics.** If you could talk about anything, what would it be? Add as many ideas as you can to the list so you don't have to worry about having nothing to say.
- **List role models.** Who inspires you? What are they like around others? What would they do in your situation? What traits do they have that you want to develop in yourself?
- **List celebrations.** How will you celebrate every time you interact rather than isolate? (Celebrating, even in small ways, helps reduce anxiety because it releases dopamine, a feel-good chemical, into your system and reduces the stress and fear hormone cortisol).

Isolation keeps you on the outside looking in. Let your lists be your guides as you begin to join others and enrich your life.

24. Learn the Nature of Your Anxiety to Get Past It

WHAT IS THE NATURE OF your own anxiety? Does it have any of these traits:

- It's omnipresent, so that no matter where you go, it's always there.
- It's cold and sharp rather than warm and fuzzy.
- Sometimes it looms large, blocking your path away from it.
- It has the ability to take over your mind, your emotions, or your physical sensations within your body.
- It's a bully, harassing you relentlessly.

Anxiety is so cruel and uncomfortable that the majority of people living with anxiety become consumed with thoughts of kicking it out of their lives. You might be in a classroom or at work and realize that you are locked in a power struggle with your anxiety rather than paying attention to all of the other things happening around you. This is the nature of anxiety at work: it can keep you trapped, focused on it rather than on better things.

When you develop a new perspective on anxiety's nature, you can change the way your anxiety is as well as your response to it. For example:

- Anxiety is nothing more than a tag-along, a pesky younger sibling, which means it's the follower and I'm the leader, not the other way around.
- As the leader, I decide where I go, what I do, and how I think and feel.
- Even when it's big, anxiety isn't a physical road block. I can keep moving forward despite its presence.

Now it's your turn to understand and redefine the nature of your own anxiety.

- Using words, drawings, or both, describe what your anxiety is like.
- Study your description, rethinking what your anxiety is truly like. (If it's a bully, what lies beneath its bravado?)
- How can you use what you know about your anxiety to bypass it? For example, does it bully you because it's an attention-grabbing oaf? Decide what you can pay attention instead of anxiety, even when the bully gets louder for a while.

25. Nonjudgement

ANXIETY IS FEAR-BASED AND FEAR puts us on edge. Anxiety tells us what is dangerous and fear makes us continuously alert for problems. This hypervigilance clouds what we see and narrows the way we interpret ourselves, our classmates and coworkers, and the situations we encounter every day. Because we're on the lookout for the problems anxiety imagines, we evaluate and judge.

When we are on the lookout for what anxiety calls danger, we think in black-and-white terms: good, bad, right, wrong, better, worse, should, shouldn't, and other extremes. These are judgments. The more we judge what's going on in our day, the more we reinforce our anxiety. Anxiety grows and our ability to let go of tension and evaluations and simply go about our day shrinks.

The way out of this limiting cycle of evaluating yourself, others, and situations is to become—despite having anxiety—nonjudgmental. Judgment narrows; nonjudgment expands. Judgment increases anxiety; nonjudgment decreases it. Judging yourself harshly, calling yourself a bad parent or an annoying person, will only serve to convince you that it's true and add to your anxiety about yourself. By contrast, when you notice and interrupt your judgments and then turn your attention to what you're doing, you can reduce anxiety, tension, and stress. Begin to shift to a perspective of nonjudgment. Develop and practice some new ways of thinking.

- **Strengthen your acceptance of what is.** When you catch yourself narrowly evaluating someone or something, remind yourself, "It just is what is." You turned in a paper and are worried because you think it's bad. A classmate reviewed it and said it's good. Two different opinions, one paper. The paper, though, is what it is—nothing more than a paper. The nature of school is that it will be evaluated, but that is just one grade and not a judgment of your personal worth.

- **Focus on facts.** Judgements are opinions that form when we're anxiously looking for problems; therefore, they're not necessarily true. Seek and pay attention only to facts. Did you have a conversation with a coworker and now your anxiety is telling you that you "should have said this" or "shouldn't have said that?" Those "shoulds" and "shouldn'ts" are uninformed opinions. The fact is that you had a conversation with a coworker.

Once you begin to perceive your world and yourself nonjudgmentally, anxiety relaxes its power to force you to fearfully evaluate for danger. You are then able to live your day more peacefully.

ACTION STEP TO TAKE NOW

Make a mantra of non-judgment. Similar to an affirmation, a mantra is a statement that summarizes an important motivating principle. To remind yourself to see yourself and the world with a non-judgmental perspective, you might repeat to yourself a statement like, "Today, I am not judging," or "My mind is open, and my thoughts are neutral." Create a mantra that works for you and repeat it to yourself often.

---

26. Break It Up for Your Brain

THE BRAIN NEEDS BREAKS. THE busier and more stressed we are, the more overloaded our brain becomes. Systems within the brain and throughout the body light up and react to stress: the neocortex, responsible for higher-order thinking and processing; the limbic system, the center of emotions; the reptilian area of the brain, causing our fight-or-flight reactions; structures such as the amygdala, hippocampus, hypothalamic-pituitary-adrenal (HPA) axis, lateral septum, and brain stem. The entirety of the brain and even the adrenal glands perched atop the kidneys are involved in producing the stress hormones cortisol, adrenaline, and norepinephrine.

This flurry of agitated reactions to stress causes or increases anxiety. Because we spend so much time there—and because there are deadlines to meet, coworkers or classmates to deal with, and a myriad of other problems that pop up regularly—work and school make the brain light up and cause anxiety.

One of the most important things you can do to stop anxiety is to nurture your brain. Breaking up your day by pausing briefly to rest your brain is highly effective in enhancing your well-being and improving your day.

Notice your thoughts, emotions, and physical sensations in your body. When you notice yourself feeling increasingly anxious, having negative thoughts, and experiencing strong emotions, your brain is telling you that it needs a break. Stop what you're doing (you can do this discretely, or you can get up and move around). Do something, even if it's only for a few minutes, to calm your brain and its anxiety-causing reactions. Some work- or school-friendly things you might do:

- Take several slow, deep breaths.
- Use mindfulness to focus your senses on the present moment, noticing your surroundings without judging them, concentrating on them rather than on anxious thoughts and emotions.
- Eat a small, healthy snack (think complex carbohydrates, protein, fruits, vegetables, nuts, seeds).

- Read a chapter in a book.
- Doodle or color.
- Avoid screens, both computer and phones.

Break up your day with short rests for your brain, and you'll begin to notice less anxiety in your day.

27. Make Good Moments in Your Day

TRYING TO SLOG THROUGH THE day with anxiety attached to us bogs us down. With anxiety holding us back, preventing us from doing what we need and want to do to succeed, it's hard to have a good day. Having anxiety can make a lot of very bad days. But here's the thing: our days are just that—*our* days. Our days do not belong to anxiety. We have the power to make good moments in our days.

Anxiety interferes, but ultimately, you can determine your focus, perspective, and actions in a way that creates good moments in your day, even if anxiety is still there. It starts with noticing. Are you stuck in your anxiety, filled with negative thoughts and anxious emotions? Are you making assumptions about what others are thinking about you? Are you worrying about bad things that might happen? When you catch yourself consumed by anxiety, you give yourself the opportunity to turn your day around.

To reclaim your day and turn the bad to good, first shift your perspective away from anxiety. Plant yourself firmly in the present moment by practicing mindfulness. Take in your surroundings with your senses and focus on things you like. Noticing a poster, plant, or decoration that you find pleasing, for example, enhances positive feelings and reduces anxious ones. Focusing on small, positive things changes your thoughts and lowers anxiety a notch. This moment is better.

Build on this positive shift by reminding yourself of what's important to you. Why are you doing what you're doing? How are you living out your values despite anxiety? The answers to these questions are empowering because they expand your thoughts from anxiety to a bigger, more important picture.

With a renewed perspective that helps you shift from what makes you anxious to what gives you purpose, you can take small actions throughout the day to make more good moments. Bit by bit, you'll reclaim your days from anxiety. Good moments will become good days. Keep at it, and your good will keep going right into great.

28. Beyond Broccoli or Pudding: Choose Wisely

EVERYONE, FROM THE INFANT JUST beginning to explore her world to the centenarian still exploring his, needs to have choices. Without a say in our lives, we naturally feel trapped and anxious. Increasing your options in life can increase your sense of freedom and control.

Imagine yourself as a child. If allowed to pick between broccoli or pudding to eat with your dinner, how would you have felt? Chances are, having that choice would have made you extraordinarily happy. Sure, the happiness in the moment involved selecting veggies or dessert, but long-term happiness and freedom from anxiety comes from choices that extend far beyond broccoli or pudding.

Having choices in life is a basic human need and one that influences how much anxiety we feel. A psychiatrist by the name of William Glasser developed an approach to enhancing mental health and creating a quality life that is used to help people worldwide. Its name? Choice Theory. The premise is that, to be happy and well (including being anxiety-free), we must have choices over our fundamental needs.

Glasser taught that we all have five basic needs:

- Survival
- Love and belonging
- Power
- Freedom
- Fun

We humans have thoughts and emotions, and we know when these needs are off. We know when we feel anxious, and we know it feels miserable. Understanding that anxiety can happen when one or more of our basic needs aren't met can power us up for taking action to create change through choices.

Devoting time to reflect on how each of the five basic needs is (or isn't) being met in your life can lead to insight into what you need to do to expand your alternatives. Journaling can be very helpful here. Use words, drawings, or both to express what might be lacking and contributing your anxiety. Then, create an action plan. What changes, small at first and gradually growing, can you make to increase your freedom through choice? Your life goes far beyond food choices. Creating options for yourself will loosen your constraints and your anxiety.

ACTION STEP TO TAKE NOW

Which of the five basic needs to you feel your life is lacking most? Commit to doing something today to meet that need. How do you want it to express itself today, and what will you do to make it happen?

---

29. Hit Your Reset Button

DID YOU KNOW THAT PEOPLE have reset buttons? Did you also know that situations in our lives—including work and school—have reset buttons? If this is new information, it's probably because anxiety intercepted the memo, so you didn't see it. Anxiety prevents a lot of pertinent information from reaching the brain because it takes over and blasts its own thoughts at us.

Anxious thoughts that stop us at work or school are something like, "I made another mistake. I always screw up. I ruin everything. No wonder no one likes me here. I'm going to be fired, and then . . ." This type of anxious thinking is called "catastrophizing," or thinking that everything is a dire problem that will grow ever bigger. It's behind the feeling of impending doom that often accompanies anxiety and panic. Anxiety's catastrophic thinking is a broken record blasting through a loudspeaker; therefore, it's hard to realize that you have control to override anxiety. You have a reset button.

This figurative button allows you to give yourself a fresh start. If you're at school or work and experiencing anxiety, you can reset yourself, your thoughts, and your emotions. You can do this through mindfulness.

- Keep an object with you as a physical reminder of a reset button.
- When you feel that impending doom or notice your spiraling thoughts, hold or study the object. Note exactly how it looks, its qualities, how heavy it is, its texture, and other aspects of it.
- As you focus on your personal reset button, breathe slowly and deeply. Let worries float away as you exhale.
- Bring your attention to your present moment. Squeeze your reset button. You are moving forward. Any mistakes or blunders already happened. They're done. Now you can reset and do what you need to do right now to keep going in your day.

Doing this mindfulness activity activates your reset button by calming your anxiety enough to change your thoughts and inspire action.

30. Presentation? Get It Over With— And Survive with a Smile

THE "P" WORD IS ONE of the most terrifying words many people can hear. (Some sources claim that presentations rank a little higher than death on lists of fears.) Skipping class or calling in sick might be tempting, but such avoidance just makes presentation anxiety worse and can get you in hot water. Despite even severe anxiety, though, you can do these.

When facing a speech or presentation, try these anxiety busters:

- From the moment you learn that you have to get up in front of people and talk, begin to visualize yourself doing it and excelling at it. Picture yourself in the clothes you'll be wearing. Visualize yourself standing, gesturing, talking, using any props you'll have. Imagine yourself relaxed and confident and knowledgeable. Do this repeatedly: before bed, when you wake up, when showering, when exercising. This technique trains your mind and body to perform so that when you do it for real, you really are more relaxed, natural, and anxiety-free.

- Also practice breathing slowly and deeply so you breathe this way during the presentation. When anxious, our breathing is rapid and shallow, which can trigger a panic reaction and make anxiety skyrocket. Developing a rhythm of anti-anxiety breathing beforehand will make it easier to breathe correctly during your speech.

- Release muscle tension by moving, tensing, and relaxing your muscles.

- Use a calming lotion, oil, or spray (chamomile is good for reducing anxiety). Apply it just before the presentation, and when you breathe deeply, you'll inhale the calming essence.

- Wear something silly to remind yourself to be light (taking things too seriously causes anxiety to flare). Socks, a bracelet, and shoelaces are discreet and won't detract from your image.

These strategies can help you step over your anxiety so you can do what you have to do. Using them probably won't make you like giving speeches and presentations, but you'll survive them and smile when they're done.

31. Forget Fear. Own Your Courageous Self.

FEAR IS A RESPONSE TO a tangible threat happening now, in the present. Anxiety is worrying about something vague or imagined, and it's rooted in the past or projected into the future. While they're different from each other, they're also related. Think of your experience at school or work. Have you ever been afraid of failing? Or of giving a speech or a presentation? What about being afraid of how others will treat you? Have you ruminated about a botched interaction with someone and been afraid that you've ruined your social life? In these cases, *fear* is synonymous with *anxiety*. No matter what word you use, you can replace it with words like courage, grit, and determination.

"Fear" can be an acronym for: "False Emotions Appearing Real." To be sure, fear and anxiety are real to us, yet they are false in that anxiety plays tricks on us, manipulating our thoughts, emotions, and beliefs.

"Fear" also can also stand for "Forget Everything and Run." When we are afraid, our fight-or-flight instinct kicks in. Often, we run. Fear and anxiety can cause avoidance and isolation. Trying to forget and run away only increases anxiety.

Then there's "Face Everything and Rise." To stand up to anxiety and fear takes a tremendous amount of courage. It can be hard to see yourself as courageous when anxiety makes you feel everything but brave, but you can reclaim your identity and take pride in your courage. Here's a way to do it:

- Think about your "anyway." You keep going despite your fear. How do you do it?

- Acknowledge your grit, that thing that explains how you keep going anyway. Grit is a combination of perseverance and passion. You keep going even when it's hard, and you bounce back when fear knocks you down because you have a reason to do so.

- Grit develops your tenacity. With determination and resolve, you can face everything and rise.

With your courage, you can put an end to fear and anxiety. Not just that, but you'll boldly create the quality life you envision.

ACTION STEP TO TAKE NOW

Define your grit. List examples of your perseverance, times when you haven't given up even though it was hard. Then, make a list of your passions: things, places, ideas, and people you love.

32. Too Much Work and Not Enough Play Make Dick and Jane Stressed, Anxious, and Miserable.

"ENGAGE IN ACTIVITY FOR ENJOYMENT and recreation rather than a serious or practical purpose." This is how the online version of the Oxford English Dictionary defines play. I'd add to the definition to include play's ability to lighten our mental load, changing our focus and reducing anxiety and stress.

Play offers a unique approach to anxiety and overthinking. It lets us deal with these problems by not dealing directly with them at all. Sometimes, we just need to let go and have fun among a day riddled with anxiety. When you notice growing feelings of frustration, exhaustion, agitation, or increased anxiety, it could be a sign that you need to have some fun.

That can be easier said than done in a formal environment like work or school; that said, you absolutely can pepper bits of fun into your day. Here are some ideas for playing at work or school when you can't cartwheel around to loud rap music. Eliminate things that aggravate your anxiety and add new ideas that will soothe your frazzled brain.

- Sketch or doodle in a notebook reserved just for this. Add to it and enjoy watching it fill and evolve as time passes.
- Make origami sculptures and give them away.
- When you have a structured break time, watch funny videos and let yourself laugh.
- Read a favorite book during a break.
- Keep a deck of cards at your desk or in your backpack, and when it's appropriate, play games with people or teach yourself magic tricks (find tutorials online).
- Play with a lump of crafting clay or putty.
- Make lists of things you want to learn, places you'd like to visit, recipes you want to try, characters from movies or books you'd like to be friends with, and other such things.

Choosing to create light moments in a day of heavy ones reduces mental chaos. It also brings a sense of freedom and control to your day because, in your playful moments, you're not at anyone's mercy. Play is for enjoyment rather than practicality; as such, playing at work or school moves us away from anxiety.

33. Wound Tight with Anxiety? Unwind.

ANXIETY HITS US EVERYWHERE: THOUGHTS, emotions, and behaviors. Oh, and the body, too. We can't forget the body—sometimes it hurts too much to be able to forget it. You might experience anxiety in your:

- Head (headache)
- Jaw
- Shoulders
- Back (upper, middle, lower)
- Heart (anxiety can feel like a heart attack)
- Lungs (anxiety can mimic asthma)
- Throat (difficulty swallowing, having a "lump")
- Stomach (acid reflux, indigestion, nausea, vomiting)
- Bowels (diarrhea, constipation)
- Bladder (frequent urination, urinary tract infections)
- Joints
- Muscles anywhere in your body (cramping, stiffness)
- Eyes (blurred vision)

Your anxiety might manifest itself in these or other ways. Having anxiety on the job or in class can be especially hard on the body because not only does anxiety cause problems, you often must sit in uncomfortable chairs or stand on hard floors. It's a double whammy of discomfort that can feel unbearable. When you're wound tight with anxiety, it's important to unwind. Meet anxiety in your body and squeeze it out with progressive muscle relaxation.

You can do this exercise discreetly wherever you are, sitting or standing. As you do it, be mindful of your purpose—letting go of muscle tension and becoming more relaxed.

- Shift your attention to your feet. Wiggle your toes in your shoes. Curl your toes and squeeze. Repeat several times. Roll your ankles.
- Move up to your calves. Squeeze, hold, and release several times.

- Continue to work your way, part by part, up to the top of your head.

- Notice where you feel tension and spend extra time in those areas. Breathe deeply and picture the oxygen flowing into the tension and releasing it.

- Once you've reached your head, scan in reverse, back down to your feet. This time notice where you *aren't* tense. Stay there and visualize the relaxation spreading out to other areas of the body.

- When you're ready, return to your task at hand feeling looser.

If you've lived with anxiety for a long time, tension might seem like a permanent state. Do this exercise often to rid your body of anxiety.

34. Change Your Approach: Do You Want the Vase or the Bowl?

SOMETIMES, WE WANT ANXIETY GONE so much that, without even realizing it, anxiety becomes our main focus. We become hyperaware of our thoughts and emotions, we change our behavior, and we obsess over our anxiety. We go to work or to school, fully aware of our anxiety, and suffer through the day.

It's natural to focus on anxiety, but unfortunately, it makes it grow rather than shrink. If you're familiar with kids, you probably know that if a young child is told, "Don't touch that vase," he will eventually touch it because that's what's on his mind. However, if the same child is intercepted from touching the vase and is told with excitement, "Look at that wooden bowl over there. What do you think is in it?" he will likely have a new object on his mind and will wander away from the vase.

We are just like this with our anxiety. We want the anxiety gone, but we don't always give ourselves a new focus. We stick with the vase and ignore the bowl apparently filled with neat things. Imagine what might happen if you change your focus from the vase to the bowl?

Rather than thinking about what you *don't* want, think of what you *do* want. Close your eyes and pretend that in the distance you see a giant bowl. It's the biggest bowl you've ever seen. What could possibly be in this humongous vessel? Your curiosity is piqued, so you start to walk toward this monstrous object. At first, anxiety bogs you down, dragging behind you like a rusty old chain. But soon you hardly notice it because your attention is riveted on this bowl. The chain remains attached to you, but it doesn't bother you as much as usual. Soon, you arrive. You find a tall ladder leading all the way up to the top. You climb and climb, and when you reach the top, you investigate and see . . .

What would you see? The bowl represents your quality life. In a journal or notebook, describe in detail what's in your bowl. What will your life be like when you focus on the bowl rather than the vase?

35. Adopt a Pet Rock.

ADOPTING A PET ROCK LITERALLY or figuratively can help you stop anxiety at work or school. These small items are effective at reducing your anxiety before it spikes out of control.

The purpose of your pet rock is to pull your mind out of its anxious ruminating, slow your breathing, and induce a sense of calm. The "pet rock" can actually be any object; it doesn't have to have googly eyes or wild fur. It doesn't even have to be a rock. You simply need something that is small enough to fit in a pocket, purse, or backpack; has a texture that is pleasing to you; and is interesting to look at.

When anxiety spikes at work or school, it might be impossible to leave the scene. Or if you do leave, there will quite likely be negative consequences. Yet staying in place can be extremely difficult. Anxiety at work or school can make it difficult to concentrate. Anxious thoughts begin to race through your mind, growing enormous as you pay attention to them. You end up trapped in anxiety and can't pay attention or work properly. This is when your pet rock or other focus object will help stop anxiety so you can function well.

A focus object is a mindfulness tool. It encourages you to draw your thoughts out of your head and into the present moment. It's something tangible that you can see and touch. The more interesting it is, the more you have available to examine. Even if it's plain, though, you can note things like shape, size, weight, and color. You can also feel your object. Is it smooth? Rough? Irregular? Symmetrical? Does it have interesting texture?

Drawing your senses and attention to your pet rock or other focus object will stop your anxiety in the moment so you can keep going forward.

ACTION STEP TO TAKE NOW

Make a pet rock. Find an intriguing rock and paint it, glue small buttons or other objects to it, and otherwise make it uniquely yours. If this isn't your thing, make or find a different focus object to use. Either way, pick something now to have with you at work or school.

36. Go to Your Happy Place

IT'S A POPULAR PLACE IN movies and on TV: the Happy Place. It also sounds like the setting of a quintessential Dr. Seuss book. The idea is that visualizing ourselves in our own unique happy place—whether it's a Seussian town or any place that evokes positive feelings—helps reduce anxiety and stress as well as increase calm and contentment.

Would you be willing to consider a new kind of happy place, one with a twist? Traditional happy places work because they remove you metaphorically from an anxiety-provoking situation. This can be effective, but it also can encourage escapism and avoidance. If your anxiety flares at work or school and you escape to your happy place, you will likely calm down; however, what happens when you open your eyes and you're still at work or school?

What if you changed your happy place? What if your happy place were at work or school? Finding a happy place there could be a valuable tool to stop anxiety in its tracks. First, a glimpse of how you use a work- or school-based happy place, then, a look at why this works:

- Pick one place in your workplace or school that isn't that anxiety-provoking. It can be a hallway, a room—anything goes.

- When your anxiety flares, you can either go there and breathe slowly and use your senses to pull your thoughts into the present moment, or

- If it's not practical for you to go there, visualize it as you would any other happy place.

If work or school increases your anxiety, why on earth would you visualize it or practice mindfulness there? Doing so reduces anxiety both short- and long-term. It teaches your brain that your entire school or workplace isn't terrible; indeed, there is at least one calming place to go to. It also shows you that you don't have to escape from anxiety to be at peace, and maybe, just maybe, work and school will become true happy places.

37. Become a SCUBA Diver

YOU CAN IMPROVE YOUR WORK or school experience by channeling your inner SCUBA diver. Perhaps surprisingly, SCUBA divers don't have to know how to swim. These men and women (and even kids) who dive down into deep water must know how to maneuver and use diving equipment to stay alive and find their way back to the boat, but they don't have to know how to swim.

Imagine the possibilities if you channeled your inner diver and dove into the life you wanted before you knew that anxiety was gone. Just as a SCUBA diver begins preparing and diving before waiting to learn how to swim, you can prepare and begin living your quality life without waiting to know how to "swim" without anxiety.

Like a diver, you need equipment to propel yourself around and navigate your world. That's all the knowledge, tools, and techniques you're developing. You also need to know where you're going and why. You'll be going to work or to school, of course, but why? Why do you want to go there? What's the purpose of your "dive?" Knowing that you have a reason for going to your job or to your classes helps you propel yourself forward even though you haven't fully jettisoned anxiety.

Knowing your reason for working or getting your education helps you focus on what's important. You can then make simple goals that move you closer to bigger ones. Develop action steps to take every day to fulfill your purpose and meet goals. Anxiety may try to stop you at every turn, and when it does, return to your reason, purpose, goals, and action steps. These provide solid focal points to draw your attention away from anxiety.

If a SCUBA diver waits to dive until she learns to swim, she will miss a lot. Likewise, you could miss a lot of your life if you wait until you learn to fully eradicate anxiety before you take the plunge. As Lemony Snicket warns, "If we wait until we're ready, we'll be waiting for the rest of our lives."

38. Stop Aimlessly Wandering the Halls

WORK DAYS AND SCHOOL DAYS can seem never-ending when we live with anxiety. A day of struggling with anxiety or trying to avoid it feels like a day wasted. It can seem like we're just wandering the halls running from anxiety. We miss positive interactions, we miss doing the work we need to do, and we miss feeling anything but tired and wired. It's disheartening to be an anxiety-driven hall wanderer.

Take back your days with committed action toward your values and goals. Anxiety's days of keeping you away from your life are over the moment you start intentionally choosing your actions. Change from an anxiety-driven life to a values-driven life. Reflect on these questions, ideally in a journal or notebook, to determine what's important to you and how you're going to act to create the life you desire:

- What do you want to experience more of every day at work or school?
- What things do you do that already work? How can you do more of them?
- What are your values, ideas that are important to you?
- For each value, what goals do you have that relate to creating your life based on what you treasure?
- What can you do to achieve your goals? What actions will you take every day to stay out of the hallway and do what you need and want to do?

When you turn your attention away from anxiety, anxiety begins to lose control over you. You are better able to take charge of your days and be proactive, deciding what you want and working to achieve it, instead of running from what you don't want.

When you find yourself wandering aimlessly as you try to avoid anxiety, simply change direction and march purposefully the other way. What is your goal for the day? What steps do you need to take to accomplish it? When you choose to take purposeful action, you weaken anxiety. You're no longer in the hallway away from the action. You're in the room getting things done as your anxiety steadily shrinks.

39. Take Care of Your Physical Health to Maintain Mental Health at Work or School

HOW ARE YOU CARING FOR yourself when you're at work or school? This might seem like a strange question because we don't typically think of "work," "school," and "self-care" as fitting together. Self-care is for home, while getting thorough the day as well as we can is for work and school. Sometimes, we don't even think of taking care of ourselves because we're busy and trying to deal with anxiety. Tuning into self-care, though, is something simple we can do to decrease anxiety in our day.

The brain needs basic things to function properly:

- Water
- Nutritious food
- Oxygen
- Exercise

Create a checklist to keep at your desk, in your locker, or in your backpack. Start thinking of anxiety as communication. Often, it's your body's way of telling you that something is off. When you notice anxiety flaring, look at your checklist.

- Are you hydrated? If it's been a while since you've drunk anything, drink eight to ten ounces of water now. Keeping a water bottle with you makes this easier.

- When did you last eat? The brain needs a steady supply of nutrients to be well. Keep healthy snacks with you during your day.

- How's your breathing? When anxiety is high, it's important to take slow, deep breaths to flood your brain with oxygen-rich blood and calm the chaos inside.

- The brain also needs you to move. You probably can't carry a treadmill with you to class or your workplace, but you don't need to. Set a quiet alarm to remind you to get up and move for just a couple minutes. At school, use the time between classes to squeeze in extra movement. Rather than going from one class straight to the next, walk around a bit to get the blood flowing.

These are simple but powerful tips. Taking care of your body and brain every day can significantly reduce anxiety. Anxiety is, after all, largely brain-based, and it manifests itself in part in the body. Meeting these basic biological needs can reduce anxiety and improve your day.

40. You're the Tortoise Who Beat the Hare

YOU PROBABLY REMEMBER THE STORY of the tortoise and the hare. The tortoise got himself into a race with a hare. That was foolish on the tortoise's part; after all, hares are very fast while tortoises are not. It would have been very natural for the tortoise to have these thoughts:

- I shouldn't have gotten myself into this situation.
- I do such stupid things.
- I will look foolish and everyone will laugh at me.
- I'm worried that I won't finish.
- I'm afraid of what will happen after the race. No one will want to be around such a loser. I'll be alone.
- I'll hide in my shell and never come out.

Anxiety often causes us to think that we can't handle things and that we're stupid for even trying. Why even bother going for that promotion? The hare is better and will get it anyway. Why bother trying out for the play or the team? The hare is so much better at everything. We need to sit at work or in school tucked inside our shell, protected from our fears and avoiding worries, and not even try.

But do you remember the rest of that classic story? Despite having anxious thoughts, the tortoise raced anyway. He walked and walked and walked some more. He couldn't even see the hare because the hare took off like a shot. But that didn't matter. The hare was the hare, and the tortoise was himself. He was determined to finish the race that he started. He didn't care about the hare. He was so much more determined than the hare. The hare stopped to take a nap. The tortoise not only crossed the finish line, but he won the race—despite his anxiety about the whole thing.

You are the tortoise. Take small steps each day throughout the day and keep going ever forward despite anxiety because slow and steady wins the race.

....

ACTION STEP TO TAKE NOW

Identify something you're anxious about and draw a race course. What is at the finish line? Label obstacles you might face. Describe or draw ways you'll move steadily ahead without paying attention to that anxiety.

....

Section 3:
ANXIETY IN RELATIONSHIPS

RELATIONSHIPS ARE HARD, AND THEY can contribute to anxiety. Additionally, living with anxiety can make relationships more difficult. Worries about yourself as a partner or friend, fears about being left alone, and anxiety due to overthinking all prevent us from letting go and enjoying good moments in our relationships.

The exercises in this section can help you reduce relationship anxiety.

41. Look for Reasons to Celebrate Your Connections

FRIENDSHIP. ROMANCE. PARENT-CHILD. CO-WORKER. WE all have many different relationships, and we can set the tone for how they'll go and how much or how little anxiety they'll cause. The way to do it is rather fun: find little things about the relationships to celebrate every day.

It's about perspective. Humans, all of us, are prone to look for the negative, which leads to anxiety. When we look for the negative—often without realizing it—in people and in our relationships with those people, we see problems. Problems exist in all relationships, but if that's our primary focus, we feel increasingly worried and anxious about them.

When we shift our perspective to the positive, we change our experience with others. To be fully effective, go beyond noticing the positive to celebrating it. Celebrating is simple. Celebrating means doing small, quick things to acknowledge something good. Celebration examples:

- Buy yourself and someone you know a cup of coffee, and enjoy drinking them together.
- Create a shared playlist on a music streaming service with a friend or family member. Have fun adding songs and sharing reactions.
- Find a walking buddy and take regular walks together for exercise and companionship.
- Add to this list so it appeals to you; think of simple thing to do with people in your life to celebrate positive things you notice about your relationships.

Does celebrating like this really make a difference in reducing relationship anxiety? It does. Celebrations stimulate the brain. When you look for positive aspects of your interactions with others, the people themselves, and your own actions, and then do something to celebrate the positive, you trigger the dopamine system in your brain. This is your brain's reward system, the feel-good system. Your brain connects the positive relationship aspects you've noticed and the little celebration you do to reinforce it (your brain doesn't need a big celebration) by releasing dopamine, feeling good, and having less anxiety.

Shifting your thinking, noticing the good on purpose, and celebrating that good releases dopamine that reduces anxiety. The more you do this, the more the brain will associate its dopamine rushes with your relationships. Celebrate your way to a new, positive relationship perspective with less anxiety.

42. You Have Worth in Your Relationships. Own It!

THERE'S SOMETHING ABOUT BEING IN a relationship of any kind that provokes anxiety. We worry that we're not good enough for a relationship and that sooner or later we'll do something to ruin it. By extension, we worry about what we should or shouldn't do or say.

This type of anxious thinking can be devastating when we start to believe what we're telling ourselves. We begin to label ourselves harshly and start to feel worthless. When we feel unworthy, we tend to act like we're unworthy. We feel nervous and unsettled around others, which increases our anxiety and feelings of worthlessness. It's time to break that awful cycle!

Just because we have these thoughts doesn't mean that they're true. Meditation teacher and author Allan Lokos tells us, "Don't believe everything you think. Thoughts are just that—thoughts." How, though, do we reduce their punch and embrace the good that we have to offer?

One way to do this is through lovingkindness affirmations. Affirmations are simple statements that reinforce what's positive about you and in your life. A lovingkindness affirmation is gentle and soft; while it's a statement rather than a request, it starts with "May I . . ." We're less prone to argue with it that way. "May I recognize my worth" is easier to ponder and internalize than "I am worthy." (You are worthy, but saying it that way makes your brain want to argue and counter with a "Yes, but . . .")

Start with this short list. Write the affirmations on cards, keep them in prominent places, and read them often. The more you do, the more they'll come to replace your anxious and self-defeating thoughts so you can own your worth.

- May I accept all that I am.
- May I be gentle with my mistakes.
- May I be happy with what I do well.
- May I be at peace with myself in all my relationships.

- May I see what I do right more than what I do wrong.

Continue adding to this list, tailoring it to your own anxiety in your relationships.

43. Practice Lovingkindness for Others in Your Relationships

IT DOESN'T MATTER IF IT'S a friendship, a romantic relationship, or a work relationship. When the people in a relationship see the good in themselves and each other, the relationship is strong and satisfying. It's not without problems, of course, but those involved are supportive and able to focus on the positive even during conflict. The root of this is each one's sense of self-worth and the belief in the other person's worth, too.

We just explored enhancing your own self-worth with lovingkindness affirmations. Thinking about your partner, friend, and others with lovingkindness does multiple things. You begin to see others differently, embracing the whole person rather than homing in on their weaknesses. This increases patience and promotes understanding. It reduces anxiety on your part because you're not as focused on problems—theirs or your own. Anxiety is further reduced because you accept the worth in your friend or partner. When you can see yourself and others as having worth despite weaknesses, it's easier to simply be in the relationship. Anxiety naturally begins to ease as lovingkindness becomes an ingrained perspective.

You can use lovingkindness affirmations toward the people in your life just as you use them with yourself. True lovingkindness statements encompass yourself, those in your life, and the whole world. Just as before, you can write these down and keep them in prominent places. Some people keep cards in their vehicle, so they can look at them at stoplights; others keep them where they spend a lot of time. Alternatively, you can keep a running list on your phone. The key is to store them where you'll use them every day.

The following lovingkindness affirmations can help you start building a running list. Word them to apply to others and to yourself.

- May my partner be at ease with himself.
- May she feel comfortable relaxing with me.
- May he see how important he is to me.

- May she let go of her worries.
- May he overcome his fear of being judged.

May you view yourself and others will lovingkindness and feel calm rather than anxious.

44. What Do You Need from Your Relationships?

WE ALL HAVE FUNDAMENTAL REQUIREMENTS of our relationships, certain words, actions, and attitudes from our partners (friends and family, too). These are essential elements that make us feel nurtured and valued. Without them, the quality of our lives suffers: our physical and mental health and our sense of well-being, happiness, and satisfaction in our relationships.

Everyone has psychological requirements for their relationships. This means, of course, that our partners and others have needs, too, and that they bring them to relationships—including relationships with us. This wouldn't be a problem if everyone's needs were the same, perfectly balanced and mutually accommodating. However, because humans are complex and varied, it's impossible for two people to come into a relationship perfectly in sync. This can be both a source of anxiety and, simultaneously, the opportunity to repair anxiety in relationships.

Below is a partial list of the things we need for ourselves and in our relationships. Some might jump out at you as important, while others you might dismiss with a shrug because they don't matter to you.

- Love
- Belonging
- Companionship
- Affection
- Power
- Autonomy/freedom
- Mutual support
- Intimacy
- Flexibility/compromise
- Fun

Anxiety can arise when you and your partner (or friend, family member, etc.) don't share many of the same needs. You might feel that your partner is unresponsive and doesn't care, and that can increase anxious thoughts ("He must hate me," "I should be a better partner," "She's judging me, and I don't measure up," "If he loved me, he'd do more things with me.")

To decrease your anxiety about your relationships, it can be helpful to contemplate what you need to feel valued in a positive relationship. Reflect in a journal or notebook. What is most important to you? Encourage your partner to do the same, and then share your top needs. Knowing each other's unique needs gives you a starting point and a place to return to when you're anxious about the relationship. How are both of your needs? Intentionally focus on your priorities to calm anxiety and strengthen your relationship.

ACTION STEP TO TAKE NOW

Sometimes, depending on others to meet our basic needs causes anxiety because we have little control over taking care of what matters most to us. List your top three relationship needs. Then, brainstorm ways you can fulfill them rather than relying on someone else.

---

45. Looking at Reality vs. Looking for Problems

ANXIETY DISTORTS THE WAY WE see ourselves and our world. It's almost as if anxiety is a virtual reality (VR) device that covers our eyes and ears and replaces our senses with its own fabricated interpretations. When we wear the VR headset, we interpret our world through the lens of anxiety.

Anxiety projects its distorted, fear- and worry-based views onto what we're experiencing. Imagine, for example, that your partner walked through the door with a slight frown and didn't talk immediately. This is a neutral event and on its own means nothing. Anxiety tells you that it most definitely means something, and it makes you look for problems through its VR headset. Distortions might include:

- He's angry about what I said this morning. What if that was the last straw, and we're through?
- I bet she looks down on me for not working hard enough. What if I disgust her?

These and other imagined, anxious thoughts get between you and the real world around you.

When you catch yourself being anxious around a friend or loved one, take off the VR glasses. Mindfulness, a strategy we've explored before starting with strategy 12, Live in Your Neutral Zone, and more recently in strategy 36, Go to Your Happy Place, as well as a few others in between, works well in this situation. When you notice your anxiety increase because you're looking for problems, try this:

- Take several slow, deep breaths.
- Fix your gaze on a focal point in front of you.
- From there, look around and notice what you see and hear.
- Don't judge. Just notice.
- Return your attention to your loved one with the same neutral observations.

When you experience someone mindfully, just as they are in the present moment, you're seeing without the VR headset. When your partner came home and was frowning and quiet, maybe he or she had a bad day, had been given a speeding ticket on the way home, had a headache, or was simply beginning to unwind after a hard day.

Anxiety makes you try to interpret people, but you can't count on it being accurate. The only thing that is accurate is what you take in through your senses, without judging, in the present moment.

46. Listen to Polonius's Advice in Shakespeare's *Hamlet*: "This above all: to thine own self be true."

INSECURITY AND ANXIETY TEAM UP to make you miserable in relationships. Each one makes the other worse. Anxiety can make you ruminate about things that are said and left unsaid. It can make you overthink how your partner acts. Then, you might begin questioning yourself, worrying that you're not good enough in your relationship. Doing so naturally increases anxiety, which in turn deepens your feelings of insecurity.

You know anxiety well. Now it's time to know yourself. You are not your anxiety. You don't exist in the context of your partner. Constantly seeing yourself in the context of someone (your partner) or something else (anxiety) is damaging because it robs you of your sense of your real self. To stop anxiety from interfering in your relationships, develop your own identity. Knowing yourself removes insecurities and reduces anxiety in your relationships.

In a journal or on your computer, begin to collect information about yourself. You want to be able to fully answer questions such as:

- Who am I?
- What's important to me?
- What are my strengths?
- What positive things do I bring to this relationship?
- What are my perfect imperfections, normal human flaws that don't make me a bad person?
- Why are my partner and I attracted to each other?
- What do my partner and I share together?
- How can I use my strengths to reduce my anxieties about my relationship?

In this exercise, focus on yourself as a unique individual. Even in the questions about your relationship and your partner, consider your own unique identity as the main idea. It's not selfish to have your own identity in a relationship; in fact, having a well-developed sense of yourself is often what chases away insecurity and anxiety.

TWO ACTION STEPS TO TAKE NOW

- In a journal or notebook reflect on the phrase, "This above all: To thine own self be true," and what it means to you.
- List five good things about yourself that you bring to your relationship. Confidently face your partner knowing that you have these things and more to offer him or her. As you add to this list, you will notice your anxiety diminish. You are beyond good enough for your relationships.

47. Drop Your Gavel

WE ALL HAVE ONE: A judging gavel. We wield it often and automatically, and it's a significant source of anxiety. Thankfully, this gavel is something we can put down. There are other things we can do with our observations than judge them.

The human brain is a natural judge, evaluating things people say and do (or don't say and don't do), analyzing our surroundings, and making decisions based on what it judges to be best.

Have you ever decided against going somewhere because you didn't want to have to talk to people and risk embarrassment? That decision to avoid is your brain's judgement that bad things will happen to you if you go to the event. It is anxiety-based, and it only serves to reinforce and increase your anxiety.

To be sure, the brain's judgments can be helpful. This gavel helps us progress toward our goals by making the right choices. Judging can keep us safe, too, helping us evaluate and avoid potential harm. Using the judging gavel becomes a problem when it halts our progress, preventing us from creating a life based on what we value. When we constantly judge what people are thinking or what is happening, we become increasingly anxious and negative. It's time to drop the gavel.

Instead of evaluating people, places, and experiences as good or bad, try:

* Imagining the possibilities: Worried that something will go wrong? Mentally list as many different outcomes (realistic and outlandish) for the situation as you can.

* Look for the good: Anxiety makes us focus on things that are wrong, whether those things are in ourselves, others, or situations. When you find yourself being negatively judgmental, switch to replacing those thoughts with positive ideas.

AN ACTION STEP TO TAKE NOW

Because even positive evaluations require a gavel, start a regular practice of observing neutrally. Look without assigning value. Right now, look around you. Mentally or on paper, note what you see without describing it. Do this two or three times every day. This simple activity teaches your brain to observe without judging.

48. You Know What They Say About Assuming . . .

WE HUMANS HAVE A QUIRKY way of listening. While we have ears designed for the task, we decide that that isn't good enough. We call in the troops: eyes for scrutinizing nonverbal communication, our thinking brain and emotional brain to find hidden meanings, memory for recalling past problems. We make assumptions, and anxiety skyrockets.

Anxiety makes us biased before any interaction begins. We assume that the person involved in any exchange is judging us negatively. We assume that he or she disapproves of us. We assume we're making mistakes and pushing him or her away. What we don't always realize is that anxiety is controlling our assumptions. Let's use Chris and Taylor as a brief example:

> **Chris:** How's your dinner? Did I make it right? (Thinking: I know it's bland and dry.)
> **Taylor:** It's good.
> **Chris (Thinking):** Taylor hates it. This is just one of many things I screw up in our relationship. I'm surprised that we're still together. I screw up at work, too. What if I get removed from the project I'm working on because I'm not good enough? I'll let everyone down, including Taylor. No wonder everyone hates me.

Not only did these assumptions increase anxiety and unhappiness that made an enjoyable dinner impossible, the anxious thoughts cascaded and pulled work into the mix. By then, Chris's anxiety was growing out of control and interfering not only with dinner but likely the rest of the night, too.

Making assumptions is also known as jumping to conclusions or mind-reading. It's an anxiety-driven thought process that feeds on itself. Just because these anxious thoughts and worries are in our head, though, it doesn't mean they're true.

The first exercise in this book was "I'm having the thought that . . ."
Now might be a great time to reread it. When you catch yourself making assumptions about what your partner/boss/coworker/friend is
thinking, stop and remind yourself that you're just having a thought.
Let your assumptions tumble away while you remain in your real life.

49. As a Parent, Do You Want Time with Your Child or Time with Anxiety?

OFTEN FROM THE MOMENT THE pregnancy test is positive, we parents worry. Anxiety is a hazard of the job, and it can wreak all sorts of havoc in your mind, body, and household. The list of things that parents worry about is seemingly endless:

- Bathroom habits and products (*The Tao of Pooh*? How about The Tao of Poo?)

- Health (Is a fever supposed to last three days?)

- Other children (Does my child have friends? Is she being bullied? Is she bullying anyone?)

- Other parents (Why does their child do so much better than mine in school and in activities? And how do I respond to their gloating about it?)

- The haunting of past mistakes (I ruined his fifth birthday party with a bad cake and stupid games. Will he be able to enjoy his sixteenth birthday tomorrow, or is he still disappointed from that disastrous party?)

- Worries about the future (What if she fails her classes? What if she can't get into college? Will she make the team? What if she develops a debilitating illness?)

These are just a few of the worries parents carry with them. We have a hard time putting them down, but the only thing that will ease all of these worries, fears, and what-ifs is to put them down. Just as it's important to lay infants and children down, it's vital to put anxiety to rest.

The most effective way to put parent anxiety to rest is to be fully present with your child and family. Pay attention to your time with them rather than to your worries by being mindful of each moment. Calm anxious thoughts by using your senses (sight, hearing, smell, touch, and even taste, when it applies). In doing this, you're making your family time more intentional and vibrant, and you're making anxiety shrink and fade because you're not paying attention to it.

Mindfulness even calms parent anxiety when you're away from your child(ren). Pay attention to each moment and continue to gently return thoughts to the present in order to shift them away from worry and onto something more peaceful, such as a family picture. Focusing on the good is a powerful way to ride your mind of the bad.

50. Dot or Blank Space: Where You Look Affects Your Relationship Anxiety

RELATIONSHIPS ARE A LOT LIKE a huge, blank canvas. The canvas is empty except for a brown blob near the side. Close your eyes for a moment and imagine this humble piece of art. What is at the forefront of your mind? Is it the empty space, or is it the brown dot? Most people concentrate on the dot. Doing so isn't a bad thing, but it does contribute to anxiety in your relationships. To reduce this anxiety, shift your attention to the blank portion of the canvas.

The dot represents those things in our relationships that cause or increase anxiety. We have anxious thoughts about ourselves, our partner, and events that have happened in the past or might happen in the future. We worry about what we said or didn't say. We try to mind-read what our partner is thinking and feeling, which causes us to assume all sorts of negative things. Fears about the future of the relationship make up that dot, too. The more we stare at it, the more vivid it becomes and the more it grows.

That dot, however, is only a portion of the canvas. It isn't the canvas itself any more than the content of your worries is your relationship. When you look at the blank space, you might notice how open and free it is. It's ready for you to become an artist and create. What is working in your relationship? What *doesn't* cause anxiety? In what circumstances *don't* you need to mind-read or ruminate about things you or your partner said or did?

ACTION STEP TO TAKE NOW

Use a piece of paper, as big as possible, or even a canvas if you'd enjoy one, to get this out in front of you where you can see it. Draw the dot (it can be anywhere) and begin to fill in your blank space with positive aspects of your relationship, either in words or in pictures. Keep it where you can gaze at it, taking in the anxiety-lowering facets on what was once incomplete space and gazing less at your anxiety.

51. It's Okay (and Necessary) to Have Relationship Expectations

SO MUCH ABOUT RELATIONSHIPS INVOLVES balance. We need to be heard, and we need to listen. We need to get our way sometimes, we need to let our partner have his or her way sometimes, and we need to compromise most of the time. It's also vital for relationship health and reduced anxiety to balance our expectations.

For our relationships (and other aspects of our lives, for that matter) to feel secure—and without significant anxiety—we need to create and practice balance. To do this, it's important to examine and nurture our expectations.

Expectations are necessary in relationships and life. To have expectations keeps you, and the relationship, strong. Just a few important expectations:

- Requiring that your partner treat you with respect
- Wanting a give-and-take relationship in which both parties give and take
- Working on developing common goals and progressing toward them together

Remember, though, that we began this chapter with balance. If we have no expectations, we risk becoming pushovers, which causes much fear and worry. Likewise, without thoughtfully considering what we expect from our relationships, our expectations can become unrealistic and anxiety-provoking in their own way. High expectations are as damaging as low expectations. When our partners can't live up to our expectations, we worry that they don't care about us, that we did something wrong to cause them to "ignore" our needs. Such anxious beliefs can quickly spiral out of control.

Making your own list of expectations can reduce relationship anxiety because you have a solid sense of what you need and how you're going to meet those needs. It also helps you see the balance. Are your expectations too low? Are they too high? Both are unrealistic and lead to anxious thoughts, emotions, and behaviors. In writing them, you can ponder them and add or remove concepts to keep your expectations and relationships in balance and your anxiety in check.

52. Balance Your Expectations with Your Partner's Expectations

RELATIONSHIP ANXIETY OFTEN HAPPENS WITH partners are unaware of (or disrespect) each other's expectations for a positive, healthy relationship. The resulting discord causes stress and anxiety. Taking time together to honestly examine your expectations and decide how to meet them will reduce relationship anxiety and increase closeness.

To balance your ideas for what is important in your relationship requires honest communication. To make this pleasant and with minimal anxiety, try these approaches:

* Create conversation starters by writing open statements on slips of paper that you'll then select from a jar and use them to have a discussion. You might include statements about hopes and dreams, goals for your relationship, worries, joys, anger, intimacy, and other key concepts. (For example, a slip might read, "To me, a financially healthy relationship . . .")

* Three keys discussion: You and your partner each write down three expectations for your relationship that you think are vital to your healthy relationship. Share them with each other and explore you can honor all of them. Feeling heard, accepted, and valued decreases relationship stress and anxiety a great deal.

53. Practice Forgiveness

SOMETIMES WE GET HURT IN our relationships. Anxiety is often a product of hurt. When our loved ones say or do something hurtful, we might respond by worrying about the future or overthinking things that have been spoken or done.

How do we find peace when we're hurt, anxious, and uncertain about our relationships? One powerful way to recover peace is to practice forgiveness. Forgiveness is healing and anxiety-reducing. It helps us move forward in our relationships, but how do we possibly do it? These suggestions can help you forgive:

- Perspective-take. We're all human, and we have reasons behind our imperfect behavior. The reasons might be minor, like being tired or hungry. Sometimes there are bigger issues behind behavior, things in our past that others may not even know about. Consider that the person who hurt you may have had a reason that had nothing to do with you. You don't have to agree with the reason or the behavior but taking a broader perspective can help you forgive.

- Focus on the positive—*your* positive. Focus on your strengths and all the good that you do. Make a list, write about them in a journal, create a collage; do something to make yourself notice and embrace your strengths. This takes the punch out of the other person's words and actions.

- Write it down and pick it apart. Dealing with the person who has hurt you is tough when you're anxious and uncertain how to move forward. Get the hurt and anxious thoughts out of your head and onto paper. Describe what happened and what it means to you. Then, step back and study it. You might dismiss issues that don't have long-term consequences. You can address the bigger issues now that they're out of your head. You couldn't control what happened, but you are in control now. When you realize this, anxiety decreases, and you gain power. When you gain power, you can forgive and move on.

Forgiving isn't about erasing. It's about letting go. Forgiveness reduces anxiety so you can work on your relationship.

54. Take a class

RELATIONSHIPS WITH FRIENDS, COWORKERS, ACQUAINTANCES, and even people in line at the grocery store can cause social anxiety. Social anxiety can make us feel judged by others—people we know very well and complete strangers. When we're around other people, we might worry about what to say and when to say it, when to talk and when to remain silent. Worries about jumping into conversations or starting new ones can send us into a corner of the room where we stand and avoid eye contact and feel embarrassed because other people are most certainly looking and laughing. Social anxiety can hurt our relationships with others as well as with ourselves when we berate ourselves for what we think are inadequacies.

Social anxiety sometimes causes us to avoid relationships with other people. While that is a tempting and an understandable reaction, avoidance doesn't lead to a quality, anxiety-free life. In fact, it fuels fears and worries, which lead to continued escaping. It can be difficult to break out of the cycle, but it's possible. To reduce anxiety in social relationships, take a class.

Most communities offer a plethora of classes for teens and adults. Art, knitting or crocheting, photography, pottery, music, stargazing—the sky is the limit in many communities. You can join a class by yourself or with someone you know.

Classes quell relationship anxiety because you're in a setting where everyone is focused on learning and doing something. Participants tend to concentrate on the instructor and any tasks involved. Some people might talk quietly with each other while others are too engrossed in the event to talk. Being with others in a setting where everyone is focused on learning something frees you to begin to be yourself. Taking a class lets you have social relationships in a low-pressured way with the focus off you.

ACTION STEP TO TAKE NOW

Find one-time classes or courses with multiple sessions by checking with your city's parks and recreation center or community centers, library, colleges, newspaper, and even bulletin boards in grocery stores or coffee shops. Discover something that interests you and sign up. You'll teach your social anxiety that you can have peaceful relationships.

55. Keep Participating in Classes to Reduce Social Anxiety, Performance Anxiety, and Perfectionism, Too.

As we've just explored, joining a class can be a catalyst to reduce anxiety in social settings and relationships. Once you've taken that initial, fearful, step and attended a class, celebrate your courage and then register for more. Every program you participate in means that you're not avoiding social relationships.

Taking classes helps more than social anxiety. When you bravely attend a program to learn something new, you build confidence and self-efficacy, the experience of knowing you can do something. A lot of anxiety, both social and otherwise, relates to perfectionism and performance anxiety. A fear of disappointing others by not being good enough or of making mistakes in any type of performance (from being onstage to turning in a paper for a grade) can and does keep people stuck in anxiety.

The more group activities like classes, programs, and events you attend, the more power you gain over your social anxiety, performance anxiety, and perfectionism. Worry and fear about being judged and embarrassed begin to fade into the background as you engage in something new.

Classes are effective because they involve tools proven to reduce anxiety:

- Mindfulness. When you delve into a class, you can use the activities and the words of the instructor to ground you. Shifting your attention away from your worries about your relationships with others in the room and concentrating on your engagement in the lesson gives your mind something to do other than worry and fret.

- Learning. Learning something new sharpens the mind. Exploring an interest naturally decreases anxiety because you have something to replace worry.

- Joy. Anxiety is heavy, and it can take away happiness, the joy of just being in the world. Building knowledge and skill decreases anxiety; thus, you create space for e positive experiences.

- Flow. Flow refers to being so engaged in what you're doing that all other thoughts drift away without you even realizing it. Flow creates many positive emotions, including joy. It's a bit like mindfulness, too, because when you're in a state of flow, your entire being is focused on one thing. That thing isn't anxiety or relationships.

- Efficacy. The more success you have in staying in a class and determining how you want to interact with others there, the less you'll worry about being judged for mistakes.

The more you participate in the world around you, the more you'll conquer your anxiety and become at ease in your relationships with others. Anxiety can't be at the forefront when you're busy having fun and learning what might become a passion.

56. Choose Wisely

PERHAPS YOU'VE HEARD A VERSION of the line from Harper Lee's *To Kill a Mockingbird*: "'Aunty,' Jem spoke up, 'Atticus says you can choose your friends but you sho' can't choose your family . . .'"

We don't choose many of the people in our lives. This can contribute to anxiety because, unlike the friends we choose, we must deal with the unchosen ones despite dread. Anxiety strikes because we worry about interactions and their consequences. Anxiety also strikes because we feel that we don't have choices in the relationships. We're trapped.

When we feel trapped in relationships, we forget that we have choices, or we don't execute the choices we have. Instead, we feel stress, worry, and dread. Anxiety tells us that because we didn't choose a certain relationship, we have no say. That's one of anxiety's lies.

You might not be able to choose every person in your life, but you can choose how you'll respond and act:

- Choose who: Who provokes anxiety, and who inspires calm? Even in unhealthy families or other environments, it's usually possible to connect with one person. Focus on your time with him or her rather than on stressing over the less desirable people.

- Choose what and where: Regardless of how others try to make you feel, you are an independent person. Often, anxiety comes because we're afraid to set limits and boundaries. Reduce anxiety by choosing the limits you'll place on what you'll do, where you'll go, and with whom you'll do it.

- Choose why: When you have an event or gathering with difficult people, consider your greater purpose. Why will you do it (going beyond the fact that it's a requirement)? Will getting together with family or attending an event with coworkers strengthen your relationships with people you like? Will it make you feel that you did something good? Having a purpose returns control to you and releases some anxiety as a result.

Try these suggestions for a shift in perspective and action so you can choose wise responses that reduce anxiety.

57. Respond Rather Than React

ANXIETY CLOUDS OUR PERCEPTIONS. DURING a heated discussion or disagreement with another person, anxiety has a bad habit of butting in and interfering. It talks over everyone, saying things like:

- This is just like that time a while ago when he was so disrespectful.
- She's always like this. What if nothing ever changes?
- He is unreasonable. I'm never going to get through to him.
- What if this is the last straw and she leaves me? I wouldn't blame her, but I don't want to lose her.

Anxious thoughts and beliefs prevent us from fully attending to the conversation. Negative thoughts lead to emotional assumptions. Unfortunately, we react to these assumptions rather than attending to the real conversation. This can exacerbate your anxious thoughts and feelings and doesn't move you closer to resolving the issue at hand.

It's possible to quiet anxiety and have more productive conversations, even arguments, by responding in the present moment rather than reacting anxiously. When you respond, you can feel emotions like anger and disappointment, but don't act on them. A response arises from a sense of calm despite emotions.

Try these tools to get around anxiety so you can respond rather than react to others:

- Pause and take a few slow, deep breaths. This nourishes your brain with oxygen, and it provides some space for you to gather your thoughts.
- Be mindful. Ground yourself in the present moment by bringing your attention to what you can see, hear, and touch. This chases away thoughts about past issues and worries about the future.
- Now that you're more centered, respond to the meaning behind the person's words. You may need to ask him or her to repeat so you can listen fully without negative thoughts interfering.

- Responding calmly doesn't mean abandoning what's important to you. When you know you can stand up for yourself and your beliefs, it's easier to stay calm rather than reacting emotionally.

Being fully present in difficult discussions lets you think more clearly and interpret the situation for yourself rather than letting anxiety do it for you.

ACTION STEP TO TAKE NOW

Go on a mindful stroll. Practice becoming centered and attentive before you need to do so during a conversation. Breathe deeply and pay attention to the sights you see. Having thoughts is an opportunity to practice returning to your attention to what's in front of you.

58. Consider Your Sources

SOMETIMES THE RELATIONSHIPS WE HAVE with others make us feel "off" in a way we can't quite pinpoint. Some symptoms of undefined anxiety in relationships include:

- An ambiguous fear of being inadequate, of not quite measuring up
- A vague uneasiness about where you fit
- Undefined worries about being distant from others
- Feeling unsure about what good relationships "should" be

Different situations can cause this indistinct, uncomfortable anxiety in our relationships. One cause is being in a relationship that isn't right for us. Another source is that the relationships aren't fully real.

Anxiety can happen because something we're doing isn't aligned with who we are or what we value. For example, if you value a close-knit family and enjoy gathering with parents and siblings every Sunday, but your partner loathes family get-togethers, you could begin to feel that unsettled anxiety.

You can also experience this undefined anxiety on social media. These relationships feel real, and they are real—but in a limited way. We can interact with people on numerous platforms and, because we're separated by a screen, we can talk about serious, personal topics. Therefore, online relationships can feel validating. The problem is that we don't know the people we're chatting with. Comments may or may not be authentic. Also, people can post things that make their lives look so much better than our own. Some conversations are constantly negative, whether they're about personal lives or the news. Social media relationships are artificial with controlled content; thus, they can't be deeply personal. This often leads to that unclear and unsettled anxiety.

Consider this type of anxiety to be your friend. It's your mind and body warning you that the relationship in question—in person or online—might not be right for you. While every relationship has ups and downs and differences, not every relationship creates this type of anxiety. When it does happen, you might stop, listen, and evaluate whether this relationship is the right choice for you. It will help you make wise choices for your well-being.

59. To Reduce Anxiety, Establish Separate but Equal

SEPARATE BUT EQUAL HASN'T ALWAYS been a wholesome ideal in US history. (It federally sanctioned segregation in an 1896 Supreme Court ruling). However, today, the words (not the original concept) provide helpful relationship insight to decrease our anxiety about our role in important relationships.

Sometimes, partners are too close. They don't have clear boundaries between "you" and "I." They form their identity in the context of each other. Known as an enmeshed relationship, this is a situation in which both people lose their unique identity. Such a loss is a cause of high anxiety, which in turn contributes to unhealthy, unhappy relationships.

We all need well-defined senses of who we are, and we all need to feel equal—especially to our partner. We need a balanced sense of personal power. In relationships, that means that neither partner dominates or controls. Both parties share power as individuals who exist in this relationship. This creates harmony and removes the anxiety caused by discord. Both partners know that they have unique and equal roles, each equal to the other's.

Anxiety grows when partners are enmeshed or when power is unbalanced. Fear of losing oneself often creeps in, as do worries about being controlled or stifled. Anxieties around being trapped can lead to anxiety attacks. You can use these tips to become both separate and equal in your relationships:

- Discover who you are, including your strengths and values. Journal, look through magazines and make a collage out of things that speak to you, or take online inventories such as the character strengths assessment at www.viacharacter.org. Encourage your partner to do the same.
- Commit to doing something new, without your partner, at least once a month. Your partner can do something new on his or her own, too.
- Discuss your self-discoveries with each other.

- Agree to make decisions together and to listen respectfully to each other, as equals.

With awareness and intentional effort, you can become separate individuals who each has an equal say in the relationship. It's a process, but one that decreases anxiety and increases inner peace.

60. Put Down Your Tools.

WHEN WE'RE WORRIED, WE OFTEN want to fix the problem. When anxiety strikes our thoughts, emotions, physical bodies, and behaviors, we need to fix the problem. When we are anxious in our relationships, we want to fix what's happening so we can return to feeling mentally healthy and happy. Therefore, we dive in and try to fix relationship problems (including the people involved) however we can. This usually doesn't work, so our anxiety grows.

When you notice your anxiety soar and your thoughts race with worries, fears, and what-ifs about your partner and the relationship, put down your tools—your hammer, measuring tape, table saw, drill, and whatever else you have. Rather than measuring and fixing, try these practices to improve your relationship and decrease anxiety:

- Notice when you feel anxious. Write down where you were when you noticed anxiety, what you were doing and what your partner was doing, what was happening around you, the nature of your anxious thoughts, and anything else relevant.

- As you do this every time you notice anxiety strike, begin to look for patterns. Does anxiety increase at a certain time of day, with a particular activity, etc.?

- Make a list of top times anxiety strikes, recurring anxious thoughts, and people involved.

- When you encounter these prominent anxiety-provoking situations, you'll have increased awareness and gained distance between you and anxiety. Remind yourself that this is just something that happens. Breathe deeply and slowly to remain calm.

- Now that you have insight into the patterns of your anxiety, you can make some adjustments. If dinnertime is chaotic and anxiety-provoking, for example, what small changes can you make? Sometimes people act up when they're hungry. Could you make dinner a little earlier or offer healthy snacks to keep everyone level?

Adjustments aren't the same as trying to fix something. Fixing is often done blindly and hurriedly without fully understanding a problem.

Adjusting happens after you've reflected to uncover the root and patterns of anxiety in your relationships, breathing to calm down instead of reacting in a chaotic moment, and making intentional changes that replace anxiety with inner peace.

Relationships aren't easy, and they can cause significant worry and fear. You can take measures to decrease anxiety in your relationships and create well-being.

Section 4:
DAILY AND NIGHTLY WORRIES

ANXIETY IS RELENTLESS. IF WE could just have a short break from it to rest, it would be easier to manage. Unfortunately, just as moonlight can make the shadows of tree branches grow and twist, so, too, does the night transform our worries and fears into something too large and twisted to let us drift into an easy sleep.

The tips in this section will help you calm your daytime and nighttime anxiety so you and your mind can rest.

61. Distract, Distract, Distract (Squirrel!)

THE JOKE ABOUT HOW SOMETHING as irrelevant as a squirrel outside the window can cause people to easily lose focus might be more wise than funny. Anxiety, after all, steals our focus and attention. Gathering some squirrels can help us change our focus.

Anxiety grabs our attention and won't let go. The worries in our head aren't tangible, but they have a way of seeming very real. We can counter this by concentrating on what is real, outside of our head and in our life. Anxiety has our focus, but we can take it back by using distractions.

Mindfulness is a powerful tool for regaining control of your focus. As you likely remember from previous exercises, mindfulness is about using your senses to pull yourself fully into your present moment, away from your anxious thoughts. Ironically, in honing your attention, mindfulness can be the ultimate distraction. The idea is to concentrate on something other than anxiety. Think shift rather than struggle. Sometimes those squirrels outside the window are just what's needed to loosen the grip anxiety has on you.

These mindfulness activities can be the squirrels that distract you from anxiety, day or night.

- Make and use a glitter globe. Fill a small Mason jar about halfway with hot water, add a generous squeeze of glitter glue, and stir it up. Add glitter and any small objects you want to, fill the jar the rest of the way with water leaving space for things to move when you shake it. The act of making it is a distraction, and you'll have a jar to shake and distract day or night.

- Carry a distraction with you. Something that provides a physical distraction is often very effective. Place a rubber band, hair elastic, or silicone bracelet around your wrist, and when you catch yourself ruminating over worries, gently snap the band or otherwise fiddle with it.

- Listen to music or soothing nature sounds. Auditory distractions are useful, too. They're squirrels that you hear rather than see, and they're mighty diversions from anxiety.

Using distractions to divert your focus away from anxiety will, over
time, train your brain to do this naturally, before anxiety captures
your attention.

ACTION STEP TO TAKE NOW

Select something that you can keep with you to be an
instant distraction from your anxious thought, and place
it in your pocket, backpack, purse, or whatever you carry
regularly. It could be the rubber band, elastic, or bracelet
just mentioned, or it could be something else entirely. A
picture of a loved one or pet, perhaps, or a small rock to
manipulate—anything that will draw your attention.

62. Stop Feeling Guilty About Avoiding Anxiety

AVOIDANCE IS A NATURAL RESPONSE to anxiety. Too often, people who don't experience anxiety don't understand how others can avoid life. Why, they might wonder, would people need or want to avoid lunch with a group of friends or coworkers? There are myriad other examples of avoidance, all of which are equally valid.

The fact that others don't understand is merely that: a neutral fact. Becoming emotionally caught up in it by getting angry or embarrassed, or feeling guilty, keeps us stuck. Feeling guilty about avoidance does one of two things (or both):

- It increases anxiety because we're worried about how we're being judged.
- It prevents us from creating and living the life we want because we're trying to live how others think we should.

The result is a swirling storm of anxiety. We still have our original anxious thoughts, emotions, and behaviors, but in feeling guilty about avoiding people and situations, we add a mess of new anxiety. Often, this occupies our thoughts during the day and long into the night. We view the upcoming hours with dread and try to plan to get out of what we can. Guilt about avoiding things like family events, work or school obligations, and more can be overwhelming. It prevents healing because when we ruminate over guilt, we're not allowing ourselves to transcend it, move forward, and work on reducing anxiety.

Some ways to decrease guilt include:

- Acknowledge it. Facing it helps you stop trying to push away feelings of guilt or, conversely, ruminating over them. Notice guilt about avoidance, then shift your attention mindfully to the present moment. Repeat because guilt is one of those emotions that that demands your attention. The more time you spend attending to the present moment, the less intrusive guilt will become.

- Separate from past avoidance. You were doing the best you could, and now you're learning how to stop avoiding so you can move forward.

- Change your self-talk. Belittling yourself, telling yourself that you "shouldn't" increases anxiety and makes guilt stick. Removing harsh labels and commands and replacing them with positive self-observations helps reduce both guilt and avoidance.

As you work to let go of the guilt, you free yourself to reduce avoidance.

63. Stop Avoiding Your Life

IT'S TRUE THAT AVOIDANCE DOESN'T warrant guilt. Avoiding what exacerbates anxiety doesn't make you a terrible person, partner, parent, or employee. It's a coping mechanism, and sometimes by avoiding certain things, we can handle others without completely shutting down.

While avoidance isn't a character flaw, it is an unhealthy coping mechanism that limits lives—sometimes severely. Further, avoidance is a paradox: skirting feared situations may temporarily reduce anxiety; however, doing so reinforces the idea that those things should be feared. Worries continue, and anxiety skyrockets. Often, avoidance makes us remain in a state of high alert, and it expands to other situations and people. Soon, avoidance is our go-to response whenever we feel anxious, and we feel increasingly anxious because we are avoiding things.

The tragic aspect of avoidance is that it is restrictive. It limits how we live our lives, what we can (or can't) do for fun and enjoyment, and how we spend time with the people in our lives. It keeps our anxiety high and quality of life low.

The good news is that avoidance isn't part of who we are. It's merely a behavior, and behaviors can be changed. Give these approaches a try:

- Rather than avoiding what you don't want, move towards what you do want. Clearly define your goals, hopes, and dreams. The more you shift your attention to what you want, the less you'll find a need to avoid what you don't.

- Take small steps. Now that you know what you want, determine what little steps you can take every day to move toward your values and away from anxiety and avoidance.

- Do something every day that takes you a little bit out of your comfort zone. Surviving this action over and over again reduces anxiety to a nub and boosts your courage and confidence.

You have the power within you to re-enter life, to reclaim happiness, and to experience fun and lightheartedness. This leads to better days and nights because you're decreasing avoidance and anxiety while increasing the quality of your life.

64. Adopt a Beginner's Mind

ZEN BUDDHISM EMBRACES THE CONCEPT of *shoshin,* or beginner's mind. A beginner's mind is an open mind, one that isn't pre-filled with ideas. The mind of a beginner isn't a know-it-all and doesn't think it's an expert. A beginner's mind is the opposite of an anxious mind. Anxiety is bossy and controlling, and it tells you what you should worry about and what you should fear. It is closed-minded. It tries to control your actions. Anxiety often causes us to be closed to the world around us and to our very lives.

Shoshin counters anxious beliefs. With an open attitude, you experience things like:

- letting go of the need to interpret everyone and everything around you
- freedom from the fear of your preconceived notions and what might happen if they're right
- a break from relentless worries that arise out of the habit of prejudging

With intention, you can nurture a beginner's mind. Anxiety will impose its preconceived worries and what-ifs on you, but you can train your brain to be open to alternate possibilities. Use these exercises during the day and in the middle of the night:

- Cultivate curiosity. Explore new thoughts and ideas and discover new facets of the world around you. Ask questions and seek multiple answers.
- Be fully present in each moment, open to experiences rather than stuck in anxieties about the past or the future.
- Let worries go by listening to them and then adding the phrase ". . . but I don't know" after each one. This takes what anxiety says is definite and makes it indefinite.

Shoshin takes away anxiety's role of expert. Beginners can let things go because anything that might have gone wrong in the past is over. Anything that might go wrong in the future is irrelevant. The only thing that matters is the current moment, and this moment is new. This awareness induces calm during the day and fosters sleep at night.

65. Get Out of Bed

HOW MANY TIMES HAVE YOU found yourself wide awake and anxious in the middle of the night, tossing and turning or staring at the clock, watching it tick its way to morning? Here's something you can do next time anxiety tries to control your mind at night.

Get out of bed. When anxiety has you thrashing about or staring wide-eyed into the dark of your room, sometimes the best way to stop anxiety from doing that is to move. Reset your mind and body for sleep by moving to a room that you've set up for this. A room that is equipped to quiet your mind and encourage tiredness to descend over you has qualities such as:

- Dim lighting
- A comfortable chair (a chair is often preferable to a couch because lying on a couch sometimes makes you fall asleep; the quality of sleep is worse on a couch than in a bed)
- Quiet but with a way to play soothing music if you desire
- A table next to the chair to hold soothing essential oils or lotions
- A supply of relaxing activities that you can do in low lighting (like coloring, reading, knitting, playing with kinetic sand, for example)
- A glass of water

When you get up and move out of your bedroom, go right to your soothing spot. Wandering around can be too stimulating, as can turning on the television, using your computer or phone, or otherwise using something with a screen. Also avoid eating, as your body will put energy into digestion, thus keeping you awake.

When you get up and occupy your mind and senses with something calming, you shift your attention away from anxiety and allow yourself to become tired rather than wired. When you feel yourself nodding off, return to bed.

ACTION STEP TO TAKE NOW

Choose a space in your home that can help you stop anxiety in the middle of the night and get back to sleep and use the above guidelines to prepare it so it's always ready when you need it.

---

66. Simply Breathe

YOU MIGHT BE SURPRISED AT how often you hold your breath, breathe shallowly, or breathe too quickly. For most of us, breathing like this has become a habit, and a bad one at that. Such breathing aggravates the nervous system, including the brain. Slowing things down has a lasting positive impact on replacing anxiety with calm.

Proper breathing nudges the parasympathetic nervous system (PNS), the component of the nervous system responsible for slowing things down throughout the body. When the PNS receives a rich supply of oxygen in a slow fashion, it responds in kind, sending out signals of calm and reducing anxious agitation.

The brain responds to the breath, too. Scientists have identified 175 neurons that, in response to slow, deep breathing, induce relaxation. These neurons are linked to both relaxation and anxiety, and the way we breathe triggers them to signal other neurons accordingly.

These breathing techniques can help encourage the brain and the PNS to create calm, reducing anxiety in the process. Do them any time of the day or night.

- Sit or lie on your back. Place your hands gently on your belly to ensure that you're breathing deep enough for it to rise and fall. Close your eyes and inhale through your nose for five slow counts. Hold. The exhale slowly through your mouth for seven or eight slow counts. Repeat.

- Use yoga's *ujjayi*, or ocean, breath. Get comfortable, and inhale and exhale through the nose. Constrict the back of your throat slightly so your breath sounds like waves of the ocean coming in and flowing back out. Keep your breath smooth and rhythmic like the movement of waves.

- Blow bubbles. You may recall from childhood that blowing too fast against the wand doesn't produce bubbles. When your breath is deep and controlled, you can create bubbles.

Breathing isn't about removing anxiety-provoking problems from your life. It's about calming the nervous system and those 175 neurons in the brain. Intentional breathing helps in an anxious moment; furthermore, when this becomes your default way of breathing, stillness becomes your natural state of being.

67. Be an Archaeologist, and Make Throwback Thursday a Part of Your Life

ONE OF ANXIETY'S BIGGEST PITFALLS is the past. Worrying about what we said or didn't say, did or didn't do, asking "Why?" perpetuates anxiety. To reduce anxiety, we need to learn to live mindfully in the present, shifting our attention to our lives in the moment. That said, an occasional excursion into the past can dig up a treasure chest of tidbits we can use to reduce anxiety.

Think of yourself as an archaeologist rather than a traveler in a time machine. You're not in a machine to travel back and exist in the past. As an archaeologist, you're still living in the present moment and are merely a distant observer. You are seeking clues that you can use to reduce anxiety now, in your present life.

This exercise is a variation of Throwback Thursday. You're looking back to observe (not become stuck in) a time in the past when your anxiety was better. Like actual archaeology, this requires time and patience because when anxiety plagues our lives, it can seem as though we've *always* been anxious and that there was *never* a time when we were anxiety-free. This belief, though, is an automatic negative thought known as all-or-nothing or black-and-white thinking that is a common part of anxiety. No matter how it seems, we all have had times in our lives when anxiety was less than it is now. Discovering that time can help reduce anxiety in the present.

The Throwback Thursday exercise lets you channel your inner archaeologist to uncover information to make your anxiety better today.

- Visualize a time when your anxiety was better. This might require exploration, so stick with it.
- Describe that time. Write about it in a journal or notebook.
- What were you like back then? What were you doing?
- What were others like?
- What was the setting?
- What was happening in your world?

- Look for patterns an identify what was working and why.

When you've gathered information, put it to use for you. How can you do more of what worked then to improve your anxiety, and your life, now?

68. Do These Simple Daytime and Nighttime Activities to Finally Sleep

ANXIETY CAN BE A TERRIBLE night owl, preying on us while we try unsuccessfully to sleep. Anxiety impacts the brain at night, keeping neurons firing and stress hormones coursing through your system. You're left wired and tired.

Anxiety also hunts by day. While it's miserable, at least during the day we have distractions. At night, it's just us, the dark, and our anxious thoughts. While it can feel like anxiety has eaten our brains, you don't have to be a zombie. Doing certain things during the day and at night can help push anxiety out of your bed so you can sleep.

Do these things during the day to set yourself up for sleep:

- Exercise. Physical activity improves sleep.
- Drink water. Even mild dehydration affects functioning and sleep.
- Use mindfulness and distractions. Lower anxiety in the moment and reap the benefits at night.
- Eat a small, healthy snack before bed. Whole grains, unsalted nuts, protein-rich foods, and kiwis (they contain serotonin) are good choices.
- Create a simple evening ritual. Dim the lights, drink a small amount of calming tea, listen to relaxing music, or do another low-key activity. Avoid screens, as they stimulate the brain.

Do these things when anxiety keeps you awake and restless at night:

- Like you read in strategy 65, get out of bed. Move to another room so your mind breaks the association between "bed" and "anxious tossing and turning."
- Release tension with gentle stretching. Use mild movements from yoga or tai chi, or just stretch each muscle group you-style.
- Do progressive muscle relaxation. Starting at your toes, contract each muscle group. Hold for a few seconds, and then relax.

- Use aromatherapy. Breathe in essential oils, use a spritzer, or apply lotion. Lavender and chamomile are particularly calming.
- Breathe and meditate. Close your eyes, breathe slowly and deeply, and let your thoughts just come and go. Don't try to stop them, and don't hang onto them. Just concentrate on your breath.

Using these activities regularly will give you power over anxiety so you can be free by day and asleep by night.

ACTION STEP TO TAKE NOW

Select just one or two activities to start today and tonight. Do the activity (or two) for at least a week. Add just one at a time to let your brain and body get used to each little ritual.

---

69. Tell Your Worries a Story

WE ARE NOT OUR ANXIETY. Yes, there are happenings in the brain that can be a cause of anxiety, but that is separate from our identity. Likewise, we aren't our anxious thoughts and emotions. We have them, but we aren't defined by them. (If I think I'm a dog and, somehow, feel like a dog and eat from a bowl on the floor and walk on all fours, I still am not a dog. Our anxious thoughts are no different.)

Once we realize that anxiety is a problem that exists separately from us, it loses some of its power and control. A way to define yourself as separate from anxiety is to write the story of you. It's a story you'll tell your worries so they begin to understand that you're the boss. It's also a story that you write and tell yourself so you begin to understand that you're the boss.

These elements, in no particular order, help create a story that makes you grow and anxiety shrink:

- Your values. What is important to you? Include concepts, beliefs, lifestyle, people, and more.
- Your goals. These are specific things you want to achieve.
- Your dreams. What is your vision for your anxiety-free life?
- Your strengths and abilities. How do you do what you do? What will you draw on to create the quality life you desire and deserve?

Take your time developing these concepts. Find quotes, pictures, song lyrics, and other inspirational sources to help you figure out who you are at your core. What speaks to you and gets you excited? Then, put it all together into a story about who you are as a strong person who isn't his or her anxiety.

Some guidelines as you write your story:

- Spelling doesn't count.
- Have fun.
- You are a work in progress. Feel free to modify as you go.

- Read your story aloud to your anxiety and enjoy knowing that it's worried about your strength.

Storytelling has always been an integral part of the human experience. Harness it for your life.

70. Be Blissfully, Openly Aware

FEARS AND WORRIES SHRINK OUR life by narrowing thoughts and emotions. When gripped by fear of bad things that might happen, the brain goes into survival mode. The fight-or-flight mechanism kicks in and sends signals and hormones to other parts of the brain and the body. These signals control what we attend to, making us problem-focused. The more attention and energy we give to our fear and anxiety, the less we have for other aspects of our lives.

A mindfulness exercise called open awareness is helpful when fear or worry dominates your days and nights. Open awareness is a liberating exercise that loosens the grip fear and worries have on you. It creates distance between you and anxiety. When you practice open awareness, you tune in mindfully to sensory input, but you don't focus on one thing. You simply notice, and when you catch fear or worry squeezing in, you let it drift away as you return to noticing the experiences of the present moment.

You can devote special time for a regular open awareness practice, or you can engage in a short exercise anytime and anywhere you need to—or both.

General ways to be openly aware:

- Step outside. Stand, lie down, or sit in a chair. Notice, but don't stick with, sights, sounds, smells, and physical sensations. Let them come into your awareness and then drift back out. Do the same for anxious thoughts.
- When you're indoors, you can also be right where you are. Causally turn your attention to what's around you. What do you notice? What else do you notice? Let everything come and go.

Open awareness can be a very useful life skill. Whenever and wherever you are gripped by anxiety, shift your thoughts to everything around you and nothing in particular. You'll find yourself calmer and your anxious thoughts weaker and less meaningful.

71. Become a Midnight Artist

CERTAIN COMPONENTS OF ANXIETY HAVE a way of making us want to grip our hair and yank it out. One such aspect is overthinking at night. If tearing our hair out would stop the thoughts, many people would likely be on board. Overthinking when we need to sleep can become that miserable.

An anxious, overthinking mind is a chaotic, overstimulated mind. If you've ever lain in bed, fighting with the sheets, staring into the darkness seeing nothing but your anxiety, you understand how difficult it is to empty the mind. Don't tear your hair out quite yet, though, because there are things you can do to soothe the overstimulated brain. One effective tool is to become a low-key midnight artist.

Trying to force the mind to be still keeps anxiety going, but doing this activity helps the overactive mind quiet down.

How to be a low-key midnight artist:

- Move to another room. Your bedroom should be reserved for sleep.
- Turn on quiet music, preferably instrumental (lyrics can snag your brain and stuff you with new thoughts). Dim the lights.
- Depending on your preference, grab a coloring book or blank paper and colored pencils, crayons, or markers.
- Sit in a comfortable chair, wrap up in a blanket if you're cold, and begin to color or scribble to the music.
- Avoid the temptation to create, as that involves thought and can cause you to judge yourself. Just scribble. If you're coloring, give yourself permission to ignore the lines. Simply add color to the page.
- Do this to the beat and rhythm of the music to encourage your brain to let go of trying to control the process.
- Close your eyes or soften your gaze.
- Be mindful of moving your hand on the paper, changing colors, hearing the music. When anxious thoughts pop in, shift your attention back to your page, the way the colors look, and the way the music sounds.

- When you feel tired, slowly return to bed.

Channeling your midnight artist regularly will teach anxiety that you won't listen to its chatter at night.

ACTION STEP TO TAKE NOW

Set up your "studio" now. Simple is best; even a chair in a bigger room is fine. Place your materials in a bag, find a dim lamp, and have a blanket by the chair. Now, when you need this space in the night, it's ready for you.

---

72. Laugh It Off

ANXIETY IS NO LAUGHING MATTER. Its effects cause physical and emotional pain and agonizing thoughts. Nothing is funny about anxiety and what it does to us; however, laughter has an important role to play in reducing anxiety. A good belly laugh doesn't stay in the belly but has ripple effects through our entire system

Laughter decreases stress hormones and increases healthy hormones. Laughter promotes relaxation, and it releases emotions. Finding humor in our lives creates a positive shift in perspective. Anxiety keeps us mired in the negative, finding reasons to worry during the day and reminding us of them at night. Seeking humor disrupts that pattern of negativity.

Try some or all of these tricks to fill your life with laughter:

- Dance and play like a jellyfish. They lack the substance required to force themselves through the water, so they use a self-made propulsion system that lets them dance their way forward. Be a jellyfish. Move your arms like tentacles and dance around. Be silly, and laugh with yourself.

- Play funny bingo or scavenger hunt. Make a bingo card or use a sheet of paper to list your items and look for sources of laughter. See how long it takes you to complete your card or list. Add things like:

  ◇ An oddly dressed up dog

  ◇ A silly thing you saw at the grocery store, mall, theatre, park, etc.

  ◇ Funny bumper stickers

  ◇ Amusing artwork in a coffee shop, gallery, etc.

  ◇ Humorous billboards

  ◇ Add more sources of humor to provide the most benefits

- Do the above activity in reverse. Discover humorous things first and then write them down. See how long you can make your list.

- Listen to humorous podcasts or audiobooks, watch shows and movies that amuse you, take daily breaks to watch something funny on YouTube.

Laughter lurks in many places, and when you train yourself to seek it, you'll begin to find it. When you do, your perspective will begin to shift. Laugher will help you feel lighter as you chip away at anxiety's heavy presence.

73. Put Worrying on Your Agenda

WHEN YOU'RE WORKING TO GAIN control over your anxiety, you might consider setting aside a time to worry. If this sounds preposterous and off-putting, that's okay. The idea of penciling worry into our schedule is counterintuitive. If we want anxiety to go away, why would we put it on our to-do list? Because doing so helps us gain control over anxiety. This approach to stopping anxiety does two important things:

- It gives us a say in when anxiety can—and can't—jump into our life.
- It lets us acknowledge the things that worry us and then let them recede.

Our anxiety is there for a reason. The problem isn't always the worries themselves. The problem happens when anxiety takes over, bothering us relentlessly day and night; additionally, the problem grows when we try to ignore our anxiety and try (unsuccessfully) to shove it aside.

Scheduling a time to worry helps both problems. Instead of letting anxiety steamroll you all day and night, you decide when you'll think about the content of your worries. If your worry time is, say, from 2:00–2:10 but you find yourself ruminating earlier, remind yourself that you'll have time to address the problem at hand at 2:00. Then, return to what you were doing. Done consistently, this teaches your brain that it can only worry at designated times. In this way, you begin to gain the upper hand in your relationship with anxiety.

The other benefit of this is that you know that you can sit down and address your worries. Ignoring real concerns often creates more anxiety. You can address what is bothering you, but you're limited in how long you do it. This also makes you more efficient at problem-solving. Rather than infinitely worrying about a problem, you address it in brief moments at a time; therefore, you will begin to look for solutions during your worry time instead of ruminating.

Grab your planner and schedule daily times to worry. You'll add efficiency and a solution-focused mindset while decreasing anxiety and a problem-focused mindset.

74. Connect to Something Greater Than Anxiety

ONE OF THE CRUELEST THINGS that anxiety can possibly do to us is to restrict our outlook on our lives and the world around us. Anxiety attaches itself to us and, to make sure we don't look past it to find better things, it slaps blinders on us to limit what we see, creating a very narrow view of what life is all about.

Thanks to anxiety's blinders, our viewpoint is dominated by worries, what-ifs, and fears. For instance, we might receive constructive criticism on something we did. We receive many positive comments and one or two suggestions for improvement. The blinders block out the positive so we hear and remember the "negative" suggestions. Anxiety dominates our reaction and creates catastrophes and worst-case scenarios.

Happily, blinders aren't a part of our bodies; therefore, we can remove them and open our perspectives to new possibilities. Connecting to something greater than anxiety, greater even than we are, inspires us to do just that. This act of expansion is sometimes called awe, wonder, and transcendence (rising above problems). To develop a broad connection to something bigger, begin to seek and appreciate beauty. Wonder-inspiring activities include:

- Stargazing (Also, if you can't sleep, this can be a soothing activity)
- Visiting a zoo or a butterfly house
- Attending a symphony
- Hiking and enjoying the beauty of nature rather than breezing past it
- Enjoying art
- Watching professional sports and admiring the athleticism

Experiencing and building a sense of awe and wonder is enjoyable. It simply requires that we give ourselves permission to experience life and to adopt an open, mindful presence. Remove your figurative blinders and take in the world around you. See beyond your anxious thoughts, hear, smell, and feel. Replace daily worry with wonder. Let yourself come alive. When worries creep in, shift back to the awesome expanse around you, and appreciate your feelings of inner peace and joy.

ACTION STEP TO TAKE NOW

Identify something beautiful where you are. Pause and appreciate this beautiful thing for several quiet moments. Marvel at the details of it, and appreciate the whole object, too.

75. Play in the Sand

THE BRAIN AND BODY ARE intricately connected in ways that scientists are just beginning to understand. It's often called the mind-body connection; Deepak Chopra refers to it as the body-mind. Researchers have also identified what has been dubbed the brain-gut axis. This is why slow, deep, intentional breathing calms the brain and thus anxiety. It's also why our heart pounds when we're anxious. It's why blood pressure sometimes soars when we're worried, or, conversely, why we feel anxious when we have high blood pressure. The connection can explain acid reflux, muscle tension, and respiratory problems. The superhighway of nerves and blood vessels between body and brain means nothing functions in isolation.

We can use our body-mind as a tool to reduce anxiety. When anxiety strikes, we can work with the body-mind to calm it down and feel better physically and mentally.

The braided network of brain-body interaction also explains why mindfulness works. We attune to our environment with our senses (parts of the physical body), and when we use the mind to pay close attention to sensory input, our thoughts stop racing, our emotions stop roiling, and we begin to feel serene. This mindfulness can work to relieve physical symptoms of anxiety, too. Mindful movement relieves tension throughout the body. Use your body-mind during the day when anxiety is gripping you painfully and during the night when you can't sleep because of pent-up tension.

Some things you can do to release anxiety from your body are:

- Playing with sand (buy sand at a hardware store or kinetic sand from a craft store) make castles and smash them, squeeze the sand, or use a tiny rake and create a Zen garden
- Playing with raw rice: bury your hands, let it sift through your fingers, or hide small objects and search for them
- Exercising vigorously and focusing on your movement (not a recommended nighttime activity, as exercise is stimulating)

Using your physical body to release anxiety works both in the moment and over time as you reinforce the positive connection between brain and body.

76. A Tranquil Bedtime Ritual

MANY PEOPLE DESCRIBE A FRUSTRATING "tired but wired" sensation that keeps them awake at night and exhausted during the day. Sleep directly impacts quality of life. When our nights are frequently sleepless because of worries about things that happened a few hours ago or years ago, fears about of what might happen hours from now or in the distant future, and thoughts that tell us we should have done this or shouldn't have done that, daytime functioning suffers. Mentally and emotionally, we're less equipped to process the world around us and the people in it. Frustrations and anxieties grow. Bedtime arrives, and we're overtired and too keyed-up to sleep.

In times like this, the primary goal isn't to reduce anxiety. It's to fall asleep and stay asleep. The rested brain is a brain that is ready to tackle the task of anxiety reduction.

For the best sleep, begin bedtime before you crawl into bed. Your brain needs a chance to transition from rumination and worry into sleep mode. A potent method is to create and engage in a bedtime ritual.

Although a ritual is more than a routine, the fact that it is routine is helpful. When you do something regularly, your brain becomes accustomed to the activities and learns how to respond. A ritual has this component, but there is an element of meaning to it. Your personal meaning—why you choose the things you include in the ritual—adds tranquility and helps you transcend rumination and worry.

Your ritual is personal. Include anything that makes you still. You might consider incorporating these activities or changing them to match your personality:

- Go to a quiet space free from distractions. Be present there.
- Sip hot tea, and fully experience the taste, feel, aroma, steam.
- Listen to relaxing instrumental music.
- Do gentle yoga or stretching.
- Take a hot bubble bath.

- Light a candle in a dark room.
- Use an oil burner or diffuser.
- Color.
- Knit.

Quietly unwinding to close your day with peace and meaning induces the stillness you need to drift into a deep sleep.

77. Break Your Screens (Well, At Least Take a Break from Them)

WE HAVE BECOME A SCREEN-BASED culture. Anywhere you are, look around you. How many laptops do you see open with people staring intently at the screen? What about mobile phones? In homes, televisions are on, day and night. Video games often dominate downtime. Screen-based activities aren't terrible, and people who frequently have a screen in front of them aren't horrible. Overuse of screens, however, contributes to anxiety and robs us of sleep.

Monitors and screens emit a blue light that decreases the brain's production of melatonin, a hormone needed for sleep. Further, using devices and TV prevents your mind from relaxing. The content, often negative or violent, projected by those screens can be anxiety-provoking. Social media, news, games, ads, and more can clutter our mind, separate us from the physical world, and contribute to overthinking. Regaining control over our devices is one way to reduce anxiety.

We don't have to give up our devices and systems. Taking breaks and creating some balance, however, is important for brain health, sleep hygiene, and anxiety reduction. Sometimes the hardest part is knowing how to take a break and what to replace screens with. Here's the beginning of a running list of go-to activities:

- Walk around the block.
- Go on photo scavenger hunt, looking for different things each time (5 different types of plants, a half dozen amusing things, eight things that begin with "B").
- Journal.
- Read.
- Hopscotch.
- Finger paint.
- Dance.
- Learn to play an instrument.
- Hit tennis balls against a backboard.

- Start a collection.
- Cook/bake.
- Put together a puzzle.
- Build a model.
- Volunteer.
- Go to the gym.
- Take a class.
- Play with a pet.
- Hike.
- Bike.
- Garden.
- Crochet or knit.
- Learn how to sew.
- Call a friend or relative (no texting).
- Get a massage.
- Play a board game.
- Go for a drive.
- Window shop.
- Visit a zoo.
- Organize a cookie exchange.
- Make homemade Play-Doh.
- Lie on your back and make cloud pictures.
- Get a telescope.
- People-watch.

Take screen breaks during the day and stop them altogether when you begin your bedtime rituals.

ACTION STEP TO TAKE NOW

Write down three times during your typical day when you'd like to take a screen break. For each time period, select one activity you will do instead of using something electronic. Set an alarm to remind you when it's time to swap screens for something different, and when the alarm sounds, put away your phone.

78. Tune in To the Rhythm of You

WHEN GEORGE AND IRA GERSHWIN composed "I Got Rhythm" as a peppy piece for the 1930s musical *Girl Crazy*, little did they know that they were gifting generations to come with a vital reminder for well-being. We all have personal internal rhythms. When we tune in, we can use those rhythms to beat anxiety.

Our brain and body work non-stop to keep us going, but we often take this background operation for granted. We notice when we're hungry, thirsty, tired, and more. Physical sensations blip onto and off our radar day and night.

Mental functions are like this, too. We notice when we're anxious, stressed, or feeling negative emotions. It's a superficial awareness, though. We don't dance deeper into our rhythms to see the connection and use it to our advantage.

Mind and body are intricately connected, functioning as one smooth unit. Physical needs, such as the need for proper nutrition and exercise, affect anxiety levels. Anxiety, in turn, contributes to physical experiences and needs (for example, some people have increased needs to use the bathroom when they're anxious). Tune in to your rhythms to increase your awareness of your own patterns of anxiety.

The first step is to simply observe and record:

- Check in with yourself throughout your day and night.
- Keep a notebook handy to record the ebb and flow of anxiety.
- As you not anxiety, conduct a body scan and jot down any sensation (muscle tension, hunger, perspiration—anything).
- Look for patterns: what's happening when your anxiety is high? Low? In between?
- Use the patterns to adjust what you do during the day and at night.

For example, did you discover that your anxiety spikes mid-morning and afternoon when you're hungry? Try eating a small, healthy snack and see if that helps. Do you wake up anxious in the middle of the night? Are you always thirsty when this happens? Consider keeping a water bottle on your nightstand and see if hydrating your brain and body helps.

You got rhythm, and when you rock with it, you can beat anxiety.

79. In the Middle of the Night, Treat Anxiety Like a Baby

IF YOU'VE EVER BEEN WITH a baby who wakes up at night, you know that it's crucial to attend to his or her needs in a way that does not excite said baby. Once stimulated, the infant is wide-awake and ready to have fun with you. In this regard, anxiety is like a needy baby. When we awaken in the middle of the night and begin to interact with our anxious thoughts and feelings, we've connected with the baby and indicated that it's playtime.

If you'd rather sleep than toss and turn, it helps to train the baby (anxiety) that if it wakes you up in the night, you will tend to immediate needs but will not stay up and play. To reduce nighttime anxiety and fall asleep, quietly respond to your physical and emotional self.

- Do you have knots of tension? Our muscles and fibers contract in response to stress and anxiety. Notice any tense spots and gently massage those knots to relax them.

- Are you holding tension everywhere? Sometimes when anxiety is strong, it invades our whole system. Progressive muscle relaxation can help a great deal with full-body anxiety. Starting with your feet, squeeze and relax each muscle group all the way to your scalp. Visualize the anxious energy leaving your body, running through your mattress, and seeping into the floor.

- Do you need some TLC? How many times does anxiety scream at you when you awaken at night? How many times do you join in, berating yourself, ruminating, and worrying? Notice when anxiety is "playing" this way and respond softly. Move into a comfortable position and become still. Breathe slowly and deeply. Listen to your breath rather than to anxiety. Mindfully focus on one thing, such as a shadow on the wall or the feel of your blanket. When anxiety talks, rather than arguing or agreeing, let the words drift and return to mindfulness.

Kindly tending to your physical and emotional needs can quiet your mind so you can sleep again.

80. Stop and Smell the Rose Oil

YOUR NOSE KNOWS HOW TO calm anxiety. Smell is a powerful sense that can directly impact our well-being. Catching a whiff of an aroma wafting through a window on a warm, sunny day can evoke strong memories of something in our childhood. Smelling something pleasant can make us smile and feel happy—even if we're anxious in that moment.

Using smells to help reduce anxiety is called aromatherapy. Researchers are conducting studies to determine whether there is something scientific behind the mental health power of smell and, if so, how effective it is in reducing anxiety. Happily, some studies have already indicated that aromatherapy can help us manage anxiety when it's added to other activities we do to reduce anxiety.

Aromatherapy involves the use of essential oils to act on the brain and create anxiety-reducing effects. An area of the brain called the limbic system is activated when certain scent molecules reach it. The limbic system is complex and involved in functions like breathing, heart rate, blood pressure, stress responses, and emotions.

Some essential oils believed to be particularly helpful for anxiety reduction include:

- Basil (Holy, Sweet)
- Lavender
- Lemon
- Lemon balm
- Rose
- Valerian
- Ylang ylang

You can inhale oils by using a device such as an oil diffuser or burner. Some are electric, while some use a candle to warm drops of oil. You can also use lotions and other skincare products, bath products, and massage oils. Allowing ourselves time to relax quietly and breathe in calming aromas can provide welcome relief from anxiety's physical and emotional symptoms.

Whether you inhale fragrances or apply them topically, aromatherapy seems to be most effective when you intentionally make it part of a relaxing routine. Honor the entire phrase, "Stop and smell the roses." Use rose oil (or any other oil) mindfully to help your body and mind enjoy a wash of calm. Stop. Set a calming ambiance. Choose pleasing essential oils. Breathe them in slowly and deeply. Let your worries leave your mind and body as you exist, fully present, only in this moment.

81. Meditate Your Way

HUMANS HAVE BEEN MEDITATING FOR thousands of years. It's a time-honored practice of calming the mind and relaxing the body; indeed, meditation has been shown to have anxiety-reducing effects that last beyond any single meditation session.

If the idea of meditation causes your anxiety to flare, you're not alone. The picture modern society paints of what meditation "should" be can be rather intimidating; however, in reality, meditation is a highly personal practice that calms *your* daily and nightly worries in a way that is effective for *you*.

The heart of a meditation practice is learning how to be still despite anxious thoughts. This inner peace comes from learning to focus our thoughts and attention and to squelch the need to react to every anxious thought or sensation we experience. Meditation, then, is a way to focus the mind on something calming that we carry into our days and nights to stop anxiety.

The best way to meditate is to do so in a way that is helpful to you. The key to meditation for anxiety is to be in a place where you can become, over time, comfortable with your whole self. That happens when you allow yourself to be still. Thoughts will continue to come, but in meditation you aren't attached to them. You observe them and let go of them by anchoring yourself in your practice. This is the heart of meditation for anxiety relief. There are seemingly unlimited ways to meditate. Among them:

- On a mediation cushion
- In a favorite chair
- Lying in bed
- Walking mindfully outside, quickly or slowly
- Walking mindfully indoors, concentrating on the floor under your bare feet
- With serene sounds in the background
- In complete silence
- Guided, with a meditation app

- On your own, focusing on your breath
- Focusing on an image
- Focusing on an object
- Repeating an affirmation
- Visualizing your thoughts drifting away on a cloud or down a bubbling brook

No matter what method is meaningful to you, developing a regular meditation practice can help you be still even if anxiety pops into the picture.

ACTION STEP TO TAKE NOW

Start a meditation practice right away. Before reading further, meditate for three minutes (you can mediate longer if you're used to meditation). Select one of the ways to meditate listed above, set a timer, and begin. Accept that your thoughts won't become still right away. You're beginning the process, that that's what it takes for you to benefit from meditation.

Section 5:
STOP ANXIETY FOR LIFE

You can stop anxiety and replace it with inner peace by defining and creating what positive psychologists call a life worth living. You don't have to wait for anxiety to be gone before you begin. Start living the life you desire, and anxiety will diminish as you do.

The tips in this section show you how to ways to live the life you want while reducing anxiety.

82. Resistance Can Be Futile

IF YOU REFLECT ON YOUR life with anxiety, you may notice that it's been rocky and full of strife. Consider how fighting with and resisting anxiety works for you. Chances are, it doesn't solve anything and may even make anxiety worse. Resisting anxiety can be futile.

When we struggle against anxiety, arguing with and cursing it, where is our focus? It's on our anxiety. What we focus on is what strengthens and grows. When we shift our attention to something else, such as positive things that will replace our anxiety, anxiety gets smaller and things important to us get bigger.

While this might be logical, it's incomplete. *How* are we supposed to stop fighting anxiety when we want it gone? *How* are we supposed to turn our attention to something else when anxiety is so loud and demanding? We achieve this by accepting our anxiety.

Anxiety is part of the human experience; therefore, completely ridding ourselves of it doesn't work. Accepting this helps end the fight against it, which frees up time and energy so we can create positive experiences. Some of the ways to accept anxiety and move forward include:

- Approaching it as an attitude. Acceptance is a mind-set that you hone by reminding yourself that anxiety may be present, but you can move forward anyway.

- Approaching it as a behavior. A big a part of acceptance is acting in a way that supports what's important to you even if you feel anxious about it.

- Being fully, mindfully present in your moment. Use your senses and thoughts, body and mind, to ground yourself in what you're doing. When you notice anxiety, accept that it's there and turn away.

- Sitting still with your anxiety. It's a form of mediation: Breathe deeply, sit quietly and just notice thoughts and feelings that come and go, and when you become aware of anxiety, acknowledge it and turn your attention to your breath.

By accepting anxiety, you replace its control with self-control. You're in charge of what you pay attention to regardless of anxiety's presence or absence. Accept your power!

83. Don't Apply Sunscreen at the Beach

CLOSE YOUR EYES AND IMAGINE yourself on a beautiful, sandy beach on a warm, sunny day. Not wanting to burn, you dig your sunscreen out of your bag and slather it on. Before it can soak in, a gust of wind causes a miniature sandstorm that pelts you with a portion of the beach. What do you want to do about it? You could spend time (unsuccessfully) trying to brush it off. You could also dunk yourself in the water and re-apply sunscreen near your car to put space between sunscreen and sand.

Putting a gap between you and your anxiety is like putting a distance between you and the sand when applying sunscreen. It can be liberating to embrace the fact that anxiety doesn't have to stick to us. When there's space between us and anxiety, we realize that it truly isn't part of us. We're not fused to it. When anxiety isn't stuck to us, we have room to move toward our goals even though it may still be present.

These activities help you separate yourself from your anxiety:

- **I'm having the thought that**_____. In response to anxious thoughts, gently repeat this statement to reinforce that these beliefs aren't real. They're merely intangible ideas.

- **Observe your anxiety.** Study your anxiety. Note exactly how you experience anxiety physically, mentally, and emotionally. Then, when your anxiety symptoms flare, you can buffer them by reminding yourself that what you're experiencing is just a fleeting symptom, not a character trait or physical problem.

- **Create a mental picture.** What does it look like to you? You can draw it or find a picture to represent it if you'd like. Imagine it hanging out a distance away from you. If it hops onto your shoulder or gets inside your head, shake it away. Giving it a look and personality separate from you and placing it a distance away can be a strong reminder that anxiety isn't stuck to you.

Don't apply sunscreen on the beach, and don't let anxiety stick to you, claiming to be part of who you are.

84. Define Your Values

WHAT WILL YOUR LIFE BE like when anxiety is no longer a problem? If that's difficult to answer, you're not alone. Anxiety can dominate the human mind. Take back what's yours by thinking about life without anxiety. In doing so, you begin to take back control over your thoughts, feelings, and actions.

When you allow yourself to acknowledge and define how things will be without anxiety, your thoughts will expand, your life will unfurl, and your fears will diminish because you're making this unknown existence known and possible.

Start by exploring and answering the question at the beginning of this strategy: what will your life be like when anxiety is no longer a problem? The way toward boldly living life on your own terms is to know exactly what those terms are. What is important to you in life? This is a process of self-discovery that is sometimes difficult to begin. When anxiety has been in charge for a long time, putting yourself back in charge of your intentions takes patience and time. Think of this process as a joyful, light hearted one. You get to discover more about who you are and decide what is important to you. You don't even have to think about anxiety or reducing it during the process of defining your values. Get to know yourself and what's important to you in life.

Among the techniques for exploring and defining your values are:

- Journaling.
- Volunteering to see what makes you come alive
- Buying magazines or looking through them at your library; leaf through them to see what interests you
- Ponder bigger concepts like family, spirituality, health, financial stability, and other broad categories

Making time to explore and define your values helps you realize what you want in life. This leads to a new direction for your life, one that has nothing to do with what you don't want.

ACTION STEP TO TAKE NOW

Your values include your self-worth. Finish these sentences:
* I am ...
* I'm good at ...
* I bring ... to my relationships, my work, and my inter-
  actions with others.
* I have worth because ...

85. Appreciate the Beauty in Your Life

ANXIETY IS A DARK CLOUD obscuring our vision. When we see the world through the lens of anxiety, we see a distorted picture. Anxiety does make things appear terrible, but that's not a full picture of our lives. When anxiety rears its ugly head, we can change our view by finding and appreciating beauty in our lives.

Seeing beauty allows us to lift the mask anxiety places over our eyes and reminds us that there is good in our world. Look beyond your worries right now. What do you see, hear, smell, feel, and even taste that is better than anxiety? What brings a smile to your face or makes you feel a little lighter despite living with anxiety?

Intentionally seeking beauty in your world shifts your focus just enough to distract you from anxiety and appreciate the positive, little things in your life. Eventually, this practice becomes a habit, and finding beauty will be more natural than taking in your world from anxiety's perspective.

Be playful with your adventures in seeking and appreciating beauty:

- Play "I spy." Make a game of finding a certain number of objects that start with a given letter. Even little things can appeal to your sense of beauty.

- Do you hear what I hear? Go for a walk and challenge yourself to detect sounds that please you.

- Stop and smell the roses. Go to a place with roses or other flowers, such as a grocery store, flower shop, farmer's market, community garden, park, or boulevard. Pause, take in their beauty, and inhale their scents. Let yourself relax and enjoy.

- Create a collage. Thumb through magazines and catalogs to find pictures of beauty. Cut them out and glue them onto pieces of poster board to create instant, go-to beauty when you need it.

- Enjoy a photo safari. Take your camera on fun adventures. Seek beauty and photograph it. Create themed albums of recorded beauty (such as "Beauty at the park").

"Because when you stop and look around, this life is pretty amazing."
—Dr. Seuss

86. Develop Your Mental Flexibility and Embrace Your Possibilities

ANXIETY IS RIGID AND DEMANDING, with a narrow-minded and rule-based approach to thoughts, feelings, and actions. We often think in terms of "shoulds" and "musts." Additionally, we judge and criticize ourselves harshly for what we think are mistakes. Rather than arguing with or giving into anxiety, when we expand our thinking and develop psychological flexibility, we can wiggle our way out of anxiety's traps.

Psychological flexibility is the ability to think and act freely. Having psychological flexibility allows you to experience anxious thoughts and feelings without becoming caged by them. It's about possibilities. Anxious thoughts and emotions become just one alternative among others. When you develop psychological flexibility, you add "and what else?" to anxiety's chatter. It looks a bit like this:

- Anxiety: You were late for work because you're irresponsible and unreliable. People can't count on you, and they resent you for it.

- You: It's true. I can't handle this job. I should quit before I get fired.

- You with psychological flexibility: And what else is possible? I was late because I was helping my son take is project to his classroom, and I called in to let people know I'd be late. That makes me responsible.

- Anxiety: You are irresponsible. You should have left the house earlier. You can't even manage your personal time. How can you manage the demands of this job?

- You: It's true. I'm not managing anything right. I can't handle things around the house, and I can't handle my job. If I can't even get to work on time, how will I get the hard stuff done?

- You with psychological flexibility: And what else is possible here? I'm a helpful mother. I made it to work. I jumped right into the task I needed to do. I'll finish it early. Being late today was one event. I'm not irresponsible or unreliable. I won't get fired for being late today.

Anxiety makes this process difficult, so it's helpful to practice. Think of it as gentle stretching exercises for your mind. Practice listing your anxieties and worries, and then brainstorming a list of alternate possibilities for each. Asking, "And what else does this mean?" opens your mind to new ideas and possibilities so you can bend and slide away from anxiety and into your life.

87. Celebrate!

ANXIETY IS ABOUT PROBLEMS. WHETHER the issues are in the past, present, or future, anxiety is the state of being mired in what's wrong. It's a rut. Forge a path out of it by finding things that reduce your anxiety and celebrating them.

To do this requires a shift in focus to away from anxiety-provoking situations and onto the positive aspects of our days. Noticing good things happening or thoughts that aren't anxiety-based is an important first step. It helps us relearn how we think and feel. A great way to notice the good is to start a running list or a collection of items that don't make you anxious. This can be specific people or situations, or it can be activities you do like organizing drawers, reading, or running. Writing these down gives you something tangible to review and remember; however, because anxiety is often deeply ingrained within us, it can be hard to override by simply noticing and recording the positive. We often need to add to this with small celebrations.

Celebrating involves doing things to acknowledge and reinforce the positive. It helps you internalize the good and keep your focus on it. Just as the brain has a negativity bias, it has a reward center that encourages us to focus on the positive. When we do something, even something small, to celebrate the positive, the reward center lights up and releases dopamine, a powerful feel-good hormone. This beats stress and anxiety hormones like cortisol. You experience good feelings and energy that begin to chase away anxiety.

Celebration has seemingly endless possibilities. Try these, or create your own:
- Splashing in puddles
- Eating a healthy treat
- Skipping
- Playing hopscotch
- Making chalk drawings
- Reading
- Sipping coffee or tea

- Singing
- Playing with a pet
- Going on a nature hike

Celebrating the positive decreases anxiety and makes us feel lighter, happier, and mentally healthier.

88. Survive Anxiety with Meaning-Making

YOU HAVE SOMETHING THAT ANXIETY never will: the ability to create meaning in your life. You can take any situation, ponder it, and assign personal meaning to it. You can ask why, and you can answer that question. Meaning-making is liberating because it helps you break free from anxiety. We can survive great obstacles by creating meaning in our lives. Meaning is hope. It's connection. Meaning is the ability to see beyond what makes us anxious. It's things that are so important to us that we keep going because of them. Meaning is how we interpret people, situations, and experiences in our lives.

This true story illustrates the importance of meaning. Viktor Frankl was an Austrian psychologist and neurologist who spent two years in Hitler's concentration camps, moving between the worst of them. He lost much and suffered greatly. He witnessed the same in others. He also observed that some people, himself included, didn't break, and even remained positive. Curious, he investigated. He discovered that those who kept their sense of meaning and purpose despite the horrors survived psychologically, while those who did not withered.

Meaning is within you, so it's easily accessible. To live a life of meaning that trumps anxiety:

- Determine what's important, then choose actions that will get you there
- Live fully, with intention, by keeping your values and goals at the forefront
- Seek good things every day, especially when anxiety strikes
- Do things with a sense of purpose: Why are you doing what you do?
- What do you want to do more of? Less?

Living life without meaning is a source of anxiety. When you act with meaning and purpose, not only do you reduce anxiety, you increase well-being and your quality of life.

ACTION STEP TO TAKE NOW

Describe something that causes you enough anxiety to avoid the situation. What will make you face it despite your anxiety? Draw on this and commit to following through.

89. Patience is an Anxiety-Beating Virtue

"It's not that I'm so smart, it's just that I stay with problems longer."
—Albert Einstein

DESPITE HIS CLAIM, ALBERT EINSTEIN was a genius. Part of his intellectual abilities was knowing that problem-solving requires patience and perseverance. Sticking with a goal despite slow progress is one of the most potent ways to achieve that goal. Doing this is a skill that requires patience.

It's easy to grow frustrated with the process of replacing anxiety with inner peace and calm because reducing anxiety doesn't happen overnight. Anxiety is often deeply ingrained in our thoughts, feelings, and actions, so it takes time and an abundance of patience to extract it. Developing patience requires being content with our present moment so we can tolerate anxiety as we work to reduce it. Here are five ways to cultivate your patience with the process so you can get rid of anxiety step by steady step:

- Sit or slowly walk and mindfully take in the world. Let yourself become still or very slow and find joy in little things.

- Mindfully sip a cup of tea or another beverage. Concentrate on the taste, temperature, and other aspects of the experience. Sip slowly until your cup is empty.

- Spend time at a pond, lake, or river. Toss rocks gently into the water and watch the rings ripple outward until the disappear. Be fully present in the experience.

- Plant something. Take pictures to record its growth.

- Learn something new by taking a class. Notice the time it takes to learn.

- Nurture and record your growth. Keep a daily journal, and begin each entry with, "Today I made progress by_____."

We might heed the lesson from the proverb, "A watched pot never boils." Imagine yourself in your kitchen. You're starving. You need the water to boil now. You watch for signs that the water is heating, but the water just sits, doing nothing. It's only once you have turned your attention elsewhere that you notice the water has begun to boil. You can develop the patience and perseverance needed to turn away from the slowly heating pot of water and onto something else.

90. Work Off That Anxiety

YOUR GYM TEACHER MIGHT HAVE been a bit too intense, but it turns out that he or she was right to get you moving. Exercise and physical activity, say researchers, doctors, and mental health experts, is vital for our well-being. While there's much still left to be learned, experts do know this: getting up and getting active reduces anxiety in a given moment and over time.

Earlier, we explored the concept of the body-mind, or the mind-body connection. This connection means that we are one united being. Where the body goes, the mind follows and vice versa. You may recall the ability of slow, deep breathing to calm the overstimulated, anxious brain. Exercise works the same way. As we move our body, positive, anxiety-related changes occur in both body and brain:

- Muscle tension eases.
- Pent-up anxious energy is expelled.
- Endorphins flood our system, increasing energy and boosting positive feelings.
- Racing thoughts quiet as we become lost in the rhythm of movement.

Exercise helps us kick our anxiety to the curb in other ways, too. As we exercise, we develop new self-confidence. Our actions bring a belief in ourselves and our ability to take care of anxiety. Additionally, exercise facilitates sleep. Sleep repairs the brain to help it function optimally, and it equips us to handle our anxiety, keeping it in check as we continue to work to reduce it.

These tips can help you build exercise into your life and maximize its anxiety-reducing benefits:

- Exercise mindfully, experiencing the activity with all your senses, to increase its positive effects.
- Start small and keep it manageable. Experts have yet to determine what amount of exercise is enough for anxiety, but they do know that simply being active helps.
- You don't have to engage in formal classes or programs. Any physical activity counts, including cleaning your house.

- Do what brings you joy. Don't force yourself to run a 10K if you hate running. Anxiety lessens when you like what you're doing.

No matter what you do or how you do it, get moving and chase away your anxiety.

91. You Are What You Eat

IF YOU HAVE A PET, close your eyes and picture it now. Don't have one? No problem. Simply close your eyes and imagine one. You love this pet, so naturally you want it to be healthy and feel well. Do you make it happy by:

a. Treating it to chocolate and table scraps, and hydrating it with soda?

b. Feeding it quality foods with important nutrients and giving it water?

Do you treat yourself like you do your pet? We—body and brain—need proper nutrition to function at our optimal level. As researchers study nutrition and the brain, they're learning just how much the food we eat affects our brain, mental health, and anxiety.

The brain uses proteins, vitamins, minerals, essential fatty acids, and other elements to produce neurotransmitters like serotonin, dopamine, and gamma-aminobutyric acid (GABA) to regulate mood and anxiety. Every structure of the brain uses specific nutrients to keep anxiety in check. Blood sugar must be stable because spikes and dips cause it to produce and release stress- and anxiety-causing hormones like cortisol and adrenaline.

What we eat and drink can cause and worsen anxiety, or it can prevent and reduce it. Foods that may be fueling your anxiety include:

- Refined and processed foods
- Fast food
- Foods with saturated and trans fats
- Sugary foods and drinks
- Alcohol
- Caffeine

Just as food and beverages negatively affect anxiety, they help it, too. Some anxiety-reducing foods:

- Whole grains

- Proteins (especially poultry, eggs, dairy)
- B vitamins
- Antioxidants
- Omega-3 fatty acids (fatty fish, avocados, nuts, olive oil)
- Dark chocolate
- Water

We are all in control of what we eat and drink. We have choices, and those choices can help us shrink anxiety and feel great.

ACTION STEP TO TAKE NOW

Changing what you eat can be one of the most basic things you can do to help your anxiety—but it can be among the most difficult. Set yourself up for long-term success by changing gradually. Choose one thing from the top list to eliminate (or significantly reduce) and one thing from the bottom list to add. Continue this way at your own pace.

92. You Are *How* You Eat

HAVE YOU EVER SKIPPED MEALS because you don't have time? Have you stood at the counter or sat at your desk, gulping food without really tasting it? This style of dining aggravates anxiety because we're not giving our minds a break; further, we stress our digestive system and interfere with the supply of nutrients to the brain.

Introducing mindfulness into your mealtimes is an effective way to zap anxiety. Pull away from your worries and cultivate calm by focusing on your experience. When you intentionally savor the taste, smell, appearance, and texture of your food, your anxious thoughts recede into the background. Another component of mindful eating is allowing yourself to be fully present in the act. Put aside cell phones and other distractions. This way, it's just you and your food. Anxiety has less opportunity to sneak in when you're fully focused on the experience of your meal.

Try this mindful eating exercise to begin your anxiety-free eating practice:

- Breathe deeply as you slowly gather an apple, peanut butter, knives, and a plate.
- Choose an apple. If it was refrigerated, wrap your hands around it and feel the coolness. Notice the smooth skin.
- Grab the peanut butter. Feel the lid as it spins open. Put you ear to it as you turn. What does it sound like? Close your eyes and inhale deeply, enjoying the scent.
- Cut your apple into wedges. Hear the knife or apple slicer cut through the fruit. Trace your finger through the juice. Notice the scent of the apple and how it differs from the peanut butter.
- Spread the peanut butter onto the wedges, watching how it spreads and how it slides on the surface of the apple.
- As you eat, savor each bite. Chew slowly and fully taste. Note the texture.
- Play with the apple seeds you removed, poking them around with your fingers. How do they feel? How do they move?

Mindfully eating nutritious foods is an action you can take to cultivate a quality life with minimal anxiety.

93. Beat Anxiety with a Musical Beat: Create Playlists

LIKE A YOUNG CHILD VYING for attention, anxiety barges into our lives and demands our full attention. What does a toddler in need of attention do? Anything in her means to get it! She will turn up her volume until she is blasting, shouting to be heard. Isn't this pretty much what anxiety does?

As we've explored mindfulness in this book, we've seen that shifting our focus to something in the present moment can stop anxiety in its tracks. This does indeed work; however, sometimes anxiety kicks and screams so loudly and obnoxiously that being present with an object nearby doesn't quite do the trick. In those times, we can reduce anxiety by being mindfully present with songs we love.

Music is powerful. It influences our mood and energy levels. It inspires, motivates, and encourages. The brain directly responds to music; therefore, music can replace anxiety, especially when we listen to it attentively and mindfully. When it plays quietly in the background, our brain isn't as engaged, and it tends to drift back to anxious ruminations. When we make time to experience it intentionally, though, we allow our brain to listen and respond positively.

Something else that liberates and empowers you when you create playlists for anxiety is that there isn't a standard, premade anxiety playlist. The music that works to stop anxiety in any moment is music that you enjoy. Make as many playlists as you'd like to fit different symptoms and effects of anxiety. For example:

- Does anxiety make you feel defeated? What music boosts your mood?
- Does anxiety make you feel restless and on-edge? What music calms you?
- Does anxiety smash your self-confidence? What inspires you?

Music quiets anxiety, our inner tantrum-ing toddler, and allows us to dance freely.

ACTION STEP TO TAKE NOW

Find a song that makes you feel good and listen to it now. Get up and move to the beat or close your eyes and simply listen. When the song is over, create your anxiety-beating playlist and add this song.

94. To Beat Anxiety, Be Solution-Focused

ANXIETY CAN BE A GIGANTIC knot inside of us that is in the way of our ability to live our best life. It's a problem—a big one.

Two approaches to mental health therapy exist. The first is problem-focused in which people explore and attempt to remove what is wrong. The second is solution-focused (there's even an official counseling method called solution-focused brief therapy) that looks for what is already right and develops ways to expand it.

These tips can help you start approaching your anxiety from a solution-focused perspective:

- Seek exceptions to your anxiety. When are you less anxious? What's different? How can you intentionally set up more "less anxious" times?

- Step out of the past. When you're worrying about things that have already happened, change your thinking. Identify even one thing that's going well right now plus something you're looking forward to in the future.

- Adopt a slow but steady pace. List some actions you can take that build on what is already going well.

There's room for both problem and solution orientations in stopping anxiety, although looking for what's right instead of what's wrong may be the most effective way to loosen the grip anxiety has on you. You'll see that your best life is already happening in bits and pieces. Nurture the positive pieces so they grow so big they crowd out anxiety.

95. Slide Up the Scale Toward A Life Without Anxiety

ANXIETY IS QUICKSAND IN THE middle of a murky swamp (more accurately, it's the quicksand and the swamp). As you try to navigate your way out, you become tangled in vines, are bitten by mosquitos, trip over fallen branches, and stumble into the quicksand. Anxiety sucks you in, gripping your legs with its cold goo. The more you thrash to escape, the deeper you sink. Luckily, while you still have use of your arms, a rope swings down. You grab it and pull and grunt your way up out of the quicksand.

The rope is numbered from zero on one end to ten on the other end. The rope that you used to extract yourself from anxiety's quagmire is another kind of tool as well. It's a simple rating scale that empowers you to move ever forward away from your anxiety.

Scaling is component of the solution-focused approach to beating anxiety that we explored in the last segment. People use scales to rate their level of anxiety and determine what they can do to improve it.

To use this tool, draw or visualize a long, straight line. Write or picture the numbers zero to ten from left to right. Zero represents the lowest rank, the "not at all" designation, while 10 represents the other extreme. Consider these questions, and rate each on your scale:

- What is your current level of anxiety?
- What can you do right now to move that anxiety down the scale one point?

In addition to using scaling to work your anxiety down level by level, you can use it to move yourself up the scale toward your ideal life.

- Describe what your life will be like when anxiety is gone.
- On the scale, how close are you to living that life?
- What can you do today to move up the scale one point toward that one part of your ideal life?

Scaling helps change anxiety from one big, overwhelming picture to manageable steps. Use it repeatedly to keep moving in your desired direction.

96. Find Your Zest

ANXIETY CAN ROB US OF our joy and replace it with myriad worries, what-ifs, and fears. We might avoid going places or doing things because we dread feeling so anxious, or we might endure situations painfully and with difficulty. Either way, living with anxiety can make it hard to be truly happy with ourselves and our lives.

Reclaiming delight in life is possible, but it's a conundrum. Anxiety makes it difficult to fully enjoy anything. Yet it is experiencing joy that can eradicate anxiety. How do we feel joy if anxiety keeps preventing it? The words of Henri Nouwen, internationally celebrated Catholic priest and spiritual leader point the way:

"Joy does not simply happen to us. We have to choose joy and keep choosing it every day."

Joy isn't passive, nor is it always easy. Rather than waiting for anxiety to disappear so we can be happy, we create happiness so anxiety will shrink in its shadow. We must "do" happiness before we can fully feel it. The more we create pleasurable moments, the more they'll start to replace anxiety. You'll begin to feel a renewed zest for life that is liberating. How, though, do you create enjoyment and begin to live it? Let these tips guide you or inspire different ideas of your own:

- Brainstorm things that you'd love to do if anxiety weren't in your life. Go wild, because even if an idea isn't realistic, it could lead to something that is. (Starting your own Sea World in your backyard probably won't happen, but building a pond and inviting others to see it is indeed possible).

- Create a passion board. Pin drawings, words, pictures printed from magazines—anything you find inspirational or that has the potential spark excitement. This can become your go-to source for your zest.

- Do something new every day, no matter how small. Staying in your comfort zone can increase anxiety and the fear of leaving said zone, and it generates boredom.

- Read new books and articles, take classes and workshops to discover new interests.

Have fun and remember that *enjoy* is an action verb.

ACTION STEP TO TAKE NOW

Do happy, right now. What would you have fun doing in this moment? Don't judge it or dismiss it. Give yourself permission to do it regardless of how you feel.

---

97. Find Your Zen

ZEN MEANS DIFFERENT THINGS TO different people. To Zen Buddhist monks, one definition is the rigorous practice of sitting in meditation, being present through discomfort, and cultivating deep presence and awareness. To the secular crowd in our modern society, Zen can refer to yoga, the spa, or going with the flow of the moment even if it's stressful. To anyone living with anxiety, Zen often means doing something to stifle the incessant anxious chatter.

The heart of Zen for anxiety is being at peace amid hardship and struggle. As you cultivate calm, there will be less room in your mind and body for anxiety. It will shrink until it's nothing more than a speck surrounded by serene silence within.

To find your personal state of Zen and cultivate a meaningful anxiety-reducing practice, first define Zen for yourself. What does being at peace mean to you? How will you know when you've reached it? How will your life be different when your inner world is tranquil rather than tumultuous?

Now that you have a deeper understanding of what a peaceful life means to you, it's time to channel your inner monk. Because the human mind isn't naturally quiet, a Zen monk must work to instill silence and calm. What work are you willing to do to achieve it?

Develop your own Zen practice to quiet your anxious thoughts and infuse your mind and body with peace. Some ideas to get you started:

- Turn waiting times, such as red lights and long lines, into meditation opportunities, giving your attention to your breath and listening to its sound, feeling the rise and fall of your abdomen.

- Establish a small aquarium and create a daily ritual of sitting still and watching the fish. When anxiety cannon-balls in, gently turn your attention back to the fish.

- Work in your yard, feeling the earth in your hands, letting it run through the spaces between your fingers. Inhale the smell of dirt, grass, and sunshine. Smile.

Perhaps ironically, stillness comes through effort. Your own Zen practice will help you stop anxiety and start living peacefully.

98. Emergency Preparedness: Calm Mind Plan

DISASTERS HAPPEN. WE CAN'T PREVENT them, so we do the next best thing: we prepare. Depending on where we live and the nature of potential events, we might gather supplies like bottled water and canned goods, flashlights and batteries, radios, blankets, first aid kits, and extra clothing. The disaster may still strike and will likely be difficult, but we're equipped to handle it.

Anxiety itself is a bit of a disaster. It's life-disrupting and can damage our mental health and well-being. One way to survive this disaster is just like with natural disasters—by preparing and planning.

Even as your anxiety decreases because of your hard work and dedication to your quality life, it will still spike from time to time. Unfortunately, it can be hard to think and remember your anxiety-reducing tools in the midst of a tsunami of anxiety; therefore, creating a survival plan for a sudden anxiety storm will help you minimize the damage to your well-being, then clean up after it and go on with your life.

Use a dedicated notebook for recording what you'll do to calm your mind when your anxiety strikes. Include such things as:

- A list of approximately six of your favorite techniques to reduce anxiety (too few might not give you enough to draw from while too many can be overwhelming when facing a sudden spike of anxiety)
- An "evacuation" map drawing a route out of anxiety (where you go and what you do to calm yourself)
- A figurative flashlight, an object you can focus on mindfully to guide your thoughts away from What else might help you deal with a sudden attack of anxiety? The more detailed your plan, the smoother it will be to shut down the disaster before it intensifies and becomes destructive.

99. Don't Just Rid Yourself of Anxiety— Replace it with Something Better (You!)

OVERCOMING ANXIETY PRESENTS US WITH a fantastic opportunity for self-growth. Tossing anxiety out the door is only half of our goal for a life of well-being. The other half is about developing ourselves. Consider:

- Who am I? (You're not anxiety, so who, exactly, *are* you?)
- How do I want to be in my life?
- What unique strengths do I possess that I can use in my life to override anxiety? (According to the Values in Action Institute on Character, an organization devoted to supporting researchers, individuals, and professionals identify and encourage the use of unique character strengths, strengths fall into six primary categories: wisdom, courage, humanity, justice, temperance, and transcendence. Each of these contains related traits like creativity, honesty, kindness, and gratitude.)
- What will I develop within me to replace anxiety?

Engage in this reflection slowly and intentionally. Ritualize it by setting aside a specific time as often as is effective for you (Daily? Weekly?) and creating an inspiring atmosphere. Revise as needed. You're creating an empowered version of yourself. Don't rush the process.

Another helpful activity for building self-confidence and self-efficacy (the belief in your ability to be successful in what you do) is to create a jar or container for keeping track of things you do despite anxiety. On pieces of paper or large craft sticks, record the courageous things you're doing despite anxiety. You might write things like:

- I go grocery shopping.
- I went to my friend's birthday dinner.
- I'm considering volunteering to help my son's team because it's important to me.
- I drove to work on a busy highway and survived.

Without even realizing it, you do myriad things every single day even though anxiety threatens to stop you. Anxiety does stop us sometimes, but perhaps without realizing it, we stop it as well. When self-doubt creeps in or anxiety feels crushing, grab some of those papers or craft sticks and remind yourself of what you can and do accomplish.

Owning what you already do to stop anxiety and combining it with self-reflection about who you're becoming are powerful ways to be you.

ACTION STEP TO TAKE NOW

Make your jar and gather slips of paper. Doing this right away will allow you to start filling it today. Go on a scavenger hunt through your home for a jar or container that will hold a lot of slips of paper (you can change the jar later if you find something else you prefer). Place your jar, papers, and a pen or marker in a visible spot. Now, toss in the first piece of paper commemorating something you've done despite anxiety (maybe you made a courage container).

100. Live the 4 Ps: Anxiety-Stopping Virtues

IT'S EASY TO BECOME IMPATIENT and discouraged when we're trying to shake anxiety loose. We want to be free, to run and skip, not run and trip. The bad news is there are no quick fixes for overcoming anxiety. There are indeed things we can do—like deep breathing and practicing mindfulness—to reduce anxiety in a moment, but reducing it and relegating it to the background while we thrive in a quality life is a process that takes work.

The good news is that there *are* fixes for anxiety. You are equipped with inner resolve, motivation, character strengths, and an arsenal of tools and techniques to use to stop anxiety from living your life for you. You also possess four important Ps that you can draw from in the process of beating anxiety:

- Patience
- Practice
- Perseverance
- Persistence

Many things in life require the four Ps, including learning to tie shoes. A lot goes into tying shoes:

- It's an endeavor that requires mastery of about 10 steps, depending on how you count them.
- It begins with the most basic of steps, one that's often overlooked as a step: pick up the laces.
- There's a lot of fumbling and lace-dropping involved.
- If you quit, you'll be doomed to wearing Velcro tennies, and that might get old.
- If you persevere, you'll go great distances and have grand adventures with your shoes.
- Your laces might come undone, and you might trip. But no worries—you know how to tie them. Pick up those laces, retie them, double knot them, and continue forward.

Shoe-tying and anxiety-untying share commonalities. One is that each can be so frustrating that it causes tears. Further, they both are skills that require the four Ps to master. Patience is essential, practice is a must, perseverance keeps you moving toward your goal when you are frustrated and want to drop the laces and walk away in your socks, and persistence allows you to get up and keep going whenever you trip.

> "Most of the important things in the world have been accomplished by people who have kept on trying when there seemed to be no hope at all."
> —Dale Carnegie

101. Nurture Your Bloom

PICTURE A BEAUTIFUL PLANT, FLOWER, or tree. Close your eyes and study it. Look at its colors, smell its fragrance, feel the texture of different parts of the plant. Allow yourself to fully experience it and enjoy its beauty. Suddenly, you discover a seed. You're excited. You can plant brand-new foliage that will grow and enhance your home.

What are your next steps? Do you:

a. Select a beautiful pot and premium soil, carefully plant the seed at the correct depth, place it in a space with the right amount of sun, and water and fertilize it as needed?

b. Find a random container, throw in the seed, toss some dirt on top of it, stick it in a corner, and then ignore it and hope that it grows?

The seed is you. You are a beautiful human being who can bring joy to others. You can enjoy your life and blossom into who you want to be. You have the ability to beat anxiety, flourish, and grow. You have strength to take root in the quality life that you desire. The key is to treat yourself like option "a" rather than "b."

Visualize your beautiful self living a quality life free of anxiety, and then nurture yourself to grow into that life. What do you need to take care of yourself so you blossom? Look back through the book to identify some of your favorite techniques and use them as gardening tools.

To thrive, you'll need healthy roots to anchor yourself. Strengthen your roots so that even when anxiety whips up a storm, you won't break. You'll stand tall and sturdy.

You'll need branches to reach upward, welcoming your life, dreams, and goals with open arms. Those branches are also designed so that anxiety will slip right on through. You're in charge of what you hold onto and what you let go. When you realize the truth of that and the depths of its power, anxiety will lose its ability to stop you.

ACTION STEP TO TAKE NOW

Draw your beautiful self living unencumbered by anxiety.
Describe yourself in this life.

CONCLUSION

CONGRATULATIONS! HERE YOU ARE AT the end of the book. Whether you read this book in chronological order or skipped about, you've arrived at the end. That is cause to celebrate. (We've explored the notion of celebrating in a few sections of the book. If you'd like a refresher, you might thumb back to number 87, Celebrate the Positive).

As you celebrate persevering to the end of the book, sticking with it to gather strategies to keep anxiety in its place while you move forward, think of your anxiety-free life. You've had many opportunities to visualize what you and your life will be like without anxiety in the way. Let your visualizations guide you while you also remember that your life is lived one moment at a time.

As you've read throughout the book, mindfulness is empowering. Be fully present in where you are, who you're with, and what you're doing. It's in the moments when our thoughts are elsewhere that anxiety can grab hold of us and run. As you work to stop anxiety and create your life worth living, remember that we live life one moment at a time. Living moment by moment—"piece-fully" and peacefully—is one more way to stop anxiety.

> "The little things? The little moments? They aren't little."
> —Jon Kabat-Zinn

The thing that you will truly make little is your anxiety.

ADDITIONAL RESOURCES

ANXIETY MANIFESTS IN MANY WAYS. Certain elements of it are universal, such as physical and emotional symptom categories and the fact that it interferes in lives. Other components of anxiety, such as the nature of thoughts and behaviors, are unique to individuals. For this reason, mental health professionals and researchers in the field have developed and are continuing to develop a plethora of approaches to help people reduce anxiety. There is something for everyone; each and every one of us can discover what best suits us as we work to overcome our anxiety.

In this book, I've drawn from a variety of established and research-based techniques. They include:

- Mindfulness
- Acceptance and commitment therapy (ACT)
- Solution-focused therapy/Solution-focused brief therapy
- Positive psychology
- Cognitive-behavior therapy (CBT)

If you're interested in reading more about any of these anxiety-reducing approaches to mental health, these resources can get you started.

MINDFULNESS
Kabat-Zin, Jon. *Mindfulness for Beginners: Reclaiming the Present Moment—and Your Life*. Boulder, CO: Sounds True, 2012, 2016.

Mindful: Healthy Mind, Healthy Life is a useful website containing how-tos, FAQs, and a wealth of articles including a section devoted to mental health. https://www.mindful.org/

Peterson, Tanya J. *The Mindfulness Workbook for Anxiety*. Berkeley, CA: Althea Press, 2018.

ACT
Act Mindfully is an informative website offering resources that include free audio files, videos, and worksheets. https://www.act-mindfully.com.au/free-stuff/

Harris, Russ. *The Happiness Trap: How to Stop Struggling and Start Living: A Guide to ACT.* Boston: Trumpeter Books, 2008.

Peterson, Tanya J. *Break Free: Acceptance and Commitment Therapy in 3 Steps.* Berkeley, CA: Althea Press, 2016.

SOLUTION-FOCUSED THERAPY
O'Hanlon, Bill. 1999. Do One Thing Different: Ten Simple Ways to Change Your Life. New York: William Morrow and Company.

Peterson, Tanya J. 2014. "Five Solution-Focused Ways to Beat Anxiety." HealthyPlace. Accessed September 22, 2018. https://www.healthyplace.com/blogs/anxiety-schmanxiety/2014/06/five-solution-focused-ways-to-beat-anxiety

POSITIVE PSYCHOLOGY
Bohlmeijer, Ernst, and Monique Hulsbergen. *Using Positive Psychology Every Day: Learning How to Flourish.* New York: Routledge, 2018.

Seligman, Martin E.P. *Flourish: A Visionary New Understanding of Happiness and Well-being.* New York: Free Press, 2011.

The Positive Psychology Center is the official website of positive psychology at the University of Pennsylvania, where it was founded. The site provides great insights into what positive psychology is about, how it benefits people and their lives, and how to apply it. It's designed for students, professionals, and anyone interested in embracing a lifestyle of well-being. https://ppc.sas.upenn.edu/

CBT
Clark, David A., and Aaron T. Beck. *The Anxiety and Worry Workbook: The Cognitive Behavioral Solution.* New York: The Guilford Press, 2012.

Gillihan, Seth J. *Cognitive Behavioral Therapy Made Simple: 10 Strategies for Managing Anxiety, Depression, Anger, Panic, and Worry.* Berkeley, CA: Althea Press, 2018.

Positive Psychology Program. "25 CBT Techniques and Worksheets for Cognitive Behavioral Therapy." This article provides an overview of CBT, thinking patterns that can cause anxiety and other mental health struggles, and a wealth of tools, exercises, and worksheets to use. https://positivepsychologyprogram.com/cbt-cognitive-behavioral-therapy-techniques-worksheets/

BIBLIOGRAPHY

Ackerman, Courtney. 2017. "What is Solution-Focused Therapy? 3 Essential Techniques." Positive Psychology Program. Accessed September 1, 2018. https://positivepsychologyprogram.com/solution-focused-therapy/

Batthyány, Alexander. "What Is Logotherapy/Existential Analysis?" n.d. Viktor Frankl Institute. Accessed January 2018 from https://www.univie.ac.at/logotherapy/logotherapy.html

Bauer, Brent. 2017. "What Are the Benefits of Aromatherapy?" Mayo Clinic. Accessed November 2, 2018 from https://www.mayoclinic.org/healthy-lifestyle/consumer-health/expert- answers/aromatherapy/faq-20058566 Burns, David. 1999. The Feeling Good Handbook. New York: Plume.

Chödrön, Pema. 2017. "How We Get Hooked and How We Get Unhooked." *Lion's Roar*. Accessed September 19, 2018. https://www.lionsroar.com/how-we-get-hooked-shenpa-and-how-we-get-unhooked/

Chopra, Deepak, and Rudolph E. Tanzi. 2018. The Healing Self. NY: Harmony Books.

Csikszentmihalyi, Mihaly. 2016. "Mihaly Csikszentmihaly: All About Flow and Positive Psychology." Positive Psychology Program. Accessed September 21, 2018. https://positivepsychologyprogram.com/mihaly-csikszentmihalyi-father-of-flow/

Dolan, Yvonne. n.d. "What Is Solution-Focused Therapy?" Institute for Solution-Focused Therapy. Accessed September 2018. https://solutionfocused.net/what-is-solution-focused-therapy/

Duckworth, Angela. 2016. *Grit: The Power of Passion and Perseverance*. New York: Scribner.

Elliot, Brianna. 2017. "The 9 Best Foods to Eat Before Bed." Healthline. Accessed October 16, 2018. https://www.healthline.com/nutrition/9-foods-to-help-you-sleep

Estroff Marano, Hara. 2016. "Our Brain's Negative Bias: Why Our Brains Are More Highly Tuned to Negative News." *Psychology Today*. Accessed October 14, 2018. https://www.psychologytoday.com/us/articles/200306/our-brains-negative-bias

Fischer, Norman. 2017. "What Is Zen Buddhism and How Do You Practice It?" *Lion's Roar*. Accessed January 4, 2019. https://www.lionsroar.com/what-is-zen-buddhism-and-how-do-you-practice-it/

Frankl, Viktor. n.d. "The Pursuit of Happiness." Accessed January 4, 2019. https://www.pursuit-of-happiness.org/history-of-happiness/viktor-frankl/#

Frost, Robert. 1914. "A Servant to Servants." *North of Boston*. New York: Henry Holt and Co.

Glasser, William. 1998. Choice theory: A New Psychology of Personal Freedom. New York: Harper Collins.

Goldsmith, Barton. 2013. "10 Things Your Relationship Needs to Thrive." *Psychology Today*. Accessed November 26, 2018. https://www.psychologytoday.com/us/blog/emotional-fitness/201303/10-things-your-relationship-needs-thrive

Hayes, Stephen C., with Spencer Smith. 2005. *Get Out of Your Mind and Into Your Life: The New Acceptance and Commitment Therapy*. Oakland, CA: New Harbinger.

Kabat-Zinn, Jon. 2005. *Coming to Our Senses: Healing Ourselves and the World Through Mindfulness*. New York: Hachette Books.

Kline, Sarah. 2013. "Adrenaline, Cortisol, Norepinephrine: The Three Major Stress Hormones, Explained." *Huffington Post*. Accessed November 9, 2018. https://www.huffpost.com/entry/adrenaline-cortisol-stress-hormones_n_3112800

Knapton, Sara. 2017. "Deep breathing calms you down because brain cells spy on your breath." *Telegraph*: Science. March 30, 2017. Accessed December 4, 2018. https://www.telegraph.co.uk/science/2017/03/30/deep-breathing-calms-brain-cell-spy-breath/

Kornfield, Jack. n.d. "The Beauty of Beginner's Mind." Jack. Retrieved December 12, 2018 from https://jackkornfield.com/beginners-mind/

Lee, Harper. 1960. *To Kill a Mockingbird*. New York: Grand Central Publishing.

Matta, Christy. "Exercises for Non-judgmental Thinking." Psych Central. April 12, 2012. Accessed November 9, 2018. https://blogs.psychcentral.com/dbt/2010/06/exercises-for-non-judgmental-thinking/

Mayo Clinic Staff. 2017. "Depression and Anxiety: Exercise Eases Symptoms." Mayo Clinic. Accessed January 2, 2019. https://www.mayoclinic.org/diseases-conditions/depression/in-depth/depression-and-exercise/art-20046495

McDermott, Annette. 2017. "Try This: 18 Essential Oils for Anxiety." Healthline. Accessed December 11, 2018 from https://www.health-line.com/health/anxiety/essential-oils-for-anxiety

McFerrin, Bobby. 1988. "Don't Worry Be Happy." *Simple Pleasures*. EMI-Manhattan Records.

McGinley, Karson. n.d. "8 Tips for Cultivating A Beginner's Mind." The Copra Center. Retrieved December 3, 2018 from https://chopra.com/articles/8-tips-for-cultivating-a-beginners-mind

Meek, Will. 2012. "Universal Relationship Needs." *Psychology Today*. Accessed November 26, 2018. https://www.psychologytoday.com/us/blog/notes-self/201212/universal-relationship-needs

National Sleep Foundation. n.d. "Food and Drink That Promote a Good Night's Sleep." Accessed January 1, 2019. https://www.sleepfoundation.org/sleep-topics/food-and-drink-promote-good-nights-sleep

National Sleep Foundation. n.d. "Scary Ways Technology Affects Your Sleep." Accessed January 1, 2019. https://www.sleep.org/articles/ways-technology-affects-sleep/

Nordqvist, Christian. 2017. "Aromatherapy: What You Need to Know." Medical News Today. Accessed December 15, 2018. https://www.medicalnewstoday.com/articles/10884.php

Peterson, Christopher. 2006. *A Primer in Positive Psychology*. New York: Oxford University Press.

Peterson, Tanya J. 2016. *Break Free: Acceptance and Commitment Therapy in 3 Steps*. Berkeley, CA: Althea Press

Peterson, Tanya J. 2018. *The Mindfulness Workbook for Anxiety*. Berkeley, CA: Althea Press, 2018.

Power, Rhett. 2015. "11 Ways to Develop a Beginner's Mind." *Inc.* Accessed December 16, 2018. https://www.inc.com/rhett-power/11-ways-how-to-develop-a-beginner-s-mind.html

ReShel, Azriel. 2017. "Shenpa and the Art of Not Getting Hooked." Uplift. Accessed Sept. 19, 2018 from https://upliftconnect.com/shenpa-art-of-not-getting-hooked/

Robinson, Lawrence, Melinda Smith, and Jeanne Segal. 2018. "Laughter Is the Best Medicine: The Health Benefits of Humor and Laughter." HelpGuide. Accessed December 1, 2018. https://www.helpguide.org/articles/mental-health/laughter-is-the-best-medicine.htm

Schwartz, Tony. 2013. "Overcoming Your Negativity Bias." *New York Times*. Accessed October 14, 2018. https://dealbook.nytimes.com/2013/06/14/overcoming-your-negativity-bias/?_r=0

Scott, Jennifer. 2018. "The Health Benefits of Laughter." Verywell mind. Accessed December 6, 2018. https://www.verywellmind.com/the-stress-management-and-health-benefits-of-laughter-3145084

Seligman, Linda. 2006. *Theories of Counseling and Psychotherapy*, 2nd ed. Upper Saddle River, NJ: Pearson Prentice Hall.

VIA Institute on Character. n.d. "The VIA Classification of Strengths." Accessed September 17, 2018. http://www.viacharacter.org/www/Character-Strengths#

Weir, Kirsten. "The Exercise Effect." *Monitor on Psychology* 42, no. 11 (2011): 48. Accessed January 4, 2019. https://www.apa.org/monitor/2011/12/exercise.aspx